Elevating Your Origins to Love

A Guided Journey of Transformation, Healing, and Power

By Susan Drury

Published by
Hybrid Global Publishing
333 E 14th Street
#3C
New York, NY 10003

Manufactured in the United States of America, or in the United Kingdom when distributed elsewhere.

Drury, Susan.
Elevating Your Origins to Love
ISBN: 978-1-957013-33-6
eBook: 978-1-957013-34-3
LCCN: 2022906718

Cover design by: Michelle White
Copyediting by: Wendie Pecharsky
Interior design by: Suba Murugan
Author photo by: Anita Lee

www.susandrury.com

Dedicated

To my beloved parents, Joan Borden Drury and Francis Remington Drury, Jr. Thank you for bringing me into life. This is for you.

Dedicated

To my beloved parents, Joan Borden Drury and Francis Remington Drury, Jr. Thank you for bringing me into life. This is for you.

Table of Contents

How to Use This Book

You and I came onto this planet through a human body and were raised by humans. And while this is the way we all begin our journey, each gestation, each parent or caregiver, each situation and condition before, during, and after birth, influences a unique mind/body patterning within this new little person. Even a child who comes from a family with many siblings will have experiences, memories, and relationships with the other family members that are uniquely theirs.

Along with the certainties in life like taxes and death, perhaps the other true certainty is that no one person, regardless of how much they love us, can ever meet all our needs, fulfill all our desires, or spare us from the experience of pain or suffering. Regardless of how "good" or "normal" our family was, the structure of our lives is built upon a framework guaranteeing exposure to unhappiness, frustration, anger, and pain — and the resulting reactions, assumptions, and perceptions we draw from them.

This book isn't about digging into the perceived wrongs of our past or exploring just how much our parents screwed us up. It *is* about discovering how our very human bodies and nature ensure we will go through experiences, traumas, and disappointments in our earliest years for the *purpose* of setting up challenges to explore and, if we allow it, to transform and help us evolve throughout our lives. When we begin to recognize this as an appropriate and truly evolutionary paradigm, we can consciously begin to change all sorts of things for ourselves, those around us, and perhaps, in time, the planet — in the very best of ways.

The hero's journey is a mythological telling of a story where one begins from a place of ignorance and naiveté, yet embodied with untapped, unrecognized, and unrealized potential. The journey has many hardships and obstacles that will require an often-painful loss of innocence. And yet it is the hardships themselves that cultivate the hidden potentials, as the hero must courageously rise to the challenges and embrace all that their mastery requires. Only then can the hero move into full expression of all they can be.

Inherent within each of us are depths of wisdom, under-standing, and greatness. Our lives are journeys in which the difficulties we endure and encompass are the very means of our transformation; where each challenge isn't to hold us back, but to inspire us further. Regardless of your place or position in the world, you are here to walk a hero's journey.

If you feel there are negative things — habits, repetitive situations, memories, upsets, difficult relationships — that surface in your life from time to time, this book can help you gain not only insight into yourself and your familial past, but also to finally shift old, now-useless but still influential patterns.

Part of our job as humans is to move beyond what holds us stagnant in smallness and allow our lives to guide us toward greater fulfilment of purpose and expression. When we are open to healing our own misinterpreted places, we become channels of new possibility beyond just ourselves. We become the means of change for humanity and the planet itself.

As you go forward into this book, be gentle with yourself. For those who have had traumatic experiences in their early

years, tread carefully. Experiences we were not able to process, absorb, and grow beyond are akin to eating something we can't digest — let alone absorb nourishment from. The substance of it remains a stagnant toxin in our system, until we can finally break it down and render it harmless.

We can equate the depth of a trauma to the virulence of a pathogen — some make you sicker than others, requiring more time and energy to fully recover from. So anytime you feel yourself getting anxious or feeling threatened, back off a bit. We are forever growing throughout our entire lives. Nothing needs to be resolved by dinner time!

Some of you will find that reading the text and listening to the stories is enough to open up a new awareness. Others will find the guided meditations, questions, and processes helpful in transforming old stories and energies into new strength.

Go at your own pace and ignore whatever doesn't seem useful. If something resonates, then use it — and what doesn't, just walk on by. Everyone has their own best way of moving forward. There are unending opportunities to support your growth.

A Cautionary Note

One caveat — when you engage with the meditative exercises, have some quiet, uninterrupted time and space. They are designed to help you access a different brain state where you are open to receiving new insights and consciously redirecting your energies. Such work can't be done when you need to attend to other commitments.

Likewise, if you begin an exercise and notice disquieting emotions coming up, proceed gently. This isn't about blasting through protective mechanisms and reigniting long-contained traumas. Be cautious, gently probing to see where there might be old energies locked up that hold you in pain, lack, guilt, unworthiness, or danger. When met with compassionate awareness, such energies can transform into their polar opposite: joy, fulfillment, freedom, gratitude, and safety.

Make use of the questions and creative or sensory suggestions to further enhance your revelations. Writing, art, movement, imagery, and sounds can help more fully ground the changes in energetic awareness. The more we practice our changes, the more bandwidth they have within us.

You may discover that there is a place in your past — could be infancy, early or mid-childhood, even your gestation — that holds special poignancy for you. Explore that place. Don't move on too quickly. Let your intuition guide you to where you are ready for a deeper dive, and take your time. We are like onions with many layers: while you may read this book sequentially, return to any sections calling more insistently and spend some time there.

This book is a combination of memoir, human design manual, and personal transformation workbook. For the past twenty plus years, I've worked to help people evolve through their problems — physical, mental, emotional, or even spiritual — to find a new sense of wholeness for themselves. My journey into the healing profession was inspired when, at age thirty, I began to suffer from a seriously painful chronic condition called trigeminal neuralgia. Although not life-threatening in itself, the pain can make you wish you were dead. After exploring the possibilities conventional medicine could offer and finding no relief, I finally accepted that this was a mystery only I could solve. Thus began my apprenticeship in healing — both for myself and as a professional practitioner with others.

My eclectic skill set began with training in shamanic healing and cranial-sacral therapy followed by professional certification in homeopathy and the Present Child Method, all shaped within the crucible of deep psychological and spiritual discipline. Working through my own personal challenges and supporting hundreds of others along their healing path is a privilege I am deeply grateful for.

This book is a guide for anyone seeking new freedom and understanding of themselves and their humanity. Have fun with it!

Introduction

Never in history have we been so connected to the frailties and disappointments within the human global experience. Never has the prospect of humanly caused destruction, devastation, and extinction been more upfront and center in our awareness.

As humans, we are designed to bring new humans into the world. Our physiological blueprint is programmed to love and care for our children until they learn to live independently. However, a blueprint is only a template — the actual results will vary widely. And so regardless of how "normal" a childhood may have seemed, the experience perceived by each parent and child will be unique — with a full spectrum ranging from the very "goodest" to the very "baddest" — and everything in between.

This explains why so many adults, regardless of their status in life, may feel some unease when looking back at their own early years. At the parents who brought them into the world, at the conditions of their childhood, at how they were treated and at how events unfolded around them.

Conception, childbearing, birth, and child-raising are never fully within anyone's control, no matter how well-intentioned each participant is. Gaps will occur. And yet within those gaps often lie possibilities for something new — something better — to come forward.

For creation is just that — the emergence of something new out of the old. And we don't need to have a child to birth new potential into the world. Our own beingness holds all the seeds we need.

This book is designed to help you discover a new place through which you can love yourself through any feelings of trauma, disappointment, guilt, anger or regret you may still carry around your earliest years and emerge free to express more of the unique and powerful person you came here to be. Our original challenges often lay the ground for the deeper journey of our lives. Only later as adults do we discover that what disturbed us most holds the potential for our greatest fulfilment and joy.

Children seem meant to be born into challenges, and never has there been a moment where the humanly created challenges for ourselves and our planet are more pressing. And yet within us even now lies the potential of true, lasting, and positive transformation.

We must come to see our origins and ourselves in a new light. In the light of wrongs being rebirthed into rights. In the light of radical, compassionate acceptance. In the light of plain and simple love.

Open yourself to the Tao…
And everything will fall into place.[1]

---

[1] Lao-Tzu, trans. Stephen Mitchell, "Chapter 23," in Tao Te Ching: A New English Version (New York, NY: HarperPerennial, 1988.

My Beginnings

When I was born in 1957, my American parents were living in Rome. They were still newlyweds when Dad received his first overseas posting with the now long-defunct Gulf Oil Corp. Mom was already pregnant when they arrived. It was a long way from Pittsburgh, PA, but they were primed for adventure in La Dolce Vita.

It was the Roman tradition for a husband driving his laboring wife to the hospital to stick his arm out of the car window and wave a white handkerchief — whereupon everyone would immediately clear out of the way, leaning heavily on their horns. Dad was really excited about this, but Mom went into labor in the middle of a rainy December night when there wasn't a single car on the road.

The story was already off-script.

Mom was being treated by a prestigious obstetrician, best known for having delivered actress Ingrid Bergman's twins. In the current fashion, she was drugged and largely unconscious of the process happening within her own body. After birth, I was turned over to the hospital nursery, Dad went to hand out cigars at his office, and Mom was put alone into a recovery room — where over the next few hours, she hemorrhaged severely. When this was finally discovered, she heard the doctor say to the nurse, "How am I going to tell her husband that his wife has died?"

Hospitals didn't have blood available on site, so the doctor hurriedly instructed my father to go to Rome's obscurely located blood bank and bring back what she needed. He made it in the nick of time. My mother spent weeks in the hospital recovering, while I remained away in the nursery. Only when she was deemed well enough to go home did we begin our life together.

If ever there was a traumatic and disappointing birth experience, surely it was hers. She was in a foreign country, isolated from her baby, away from her husband and family at Christmastime, almost losing her life. One day a group of schoolchildren came into her hospital room to sing Christmas carols. No doubt they were surprised because instead of smiling and applauding, she burst into tears.

It was hardly the beginning of motherhood that she had expected.

When I was older and heard the story of my entrance into the world, I felt grief not only for her, but also for myself. It was bleak to consider how we missed out on that important early bonding, but Mom was hanging onto her life with no strength to care for me in my earliest days.

Did the nurses bring me down from the nursery for visits? Clearly breastfeeding couldn't happen, so we both missed out on that intimate closeness. There have been many studies showing that babies who don't bond, who are left alone for long periods of time, often don't thrive — and sometimes not even survive. But obviously we both made it through, and in pictures I've seen once we were home together, I was a well-loved baby.

But still...perhaps there are aspects of my personality that were affected, connections that didn't get fully completed because of that early separation. There are so many transitions in our lives' earliest, most helpless days, when we have left the shelter of the womb and need that loving attention.

And yet here's something that when I realized it, knocked me over. It was only after Mom passed at the great age of 94, after a long and loving relationship, that I began to consider what the alternative to our years together might have been.

She had bled heavily. The doctor thought she was going to die. How many women and babies throughout the history of humanity have been lost in childbirth? I had only ever focused on what my birth didn't provide, versus what we both so narrowly missed: her early death and me, a motherless infant, left behind. Anything missing from my first days in the world was miniscule compared to the alternative.

Welcome to the human adventure, where our challenges are laid right from the start! Losses happen and some may leave seemingly devastating marks — yet within the worst suffering, lie the seeds of our greatest growth.

What would it be like to see beyond whatever seemed wrong and discover it was just right?

What would it be like to elevate your origins to love?

PART I

Becoming Familiar With Our Neural Physiological Hardware

Knowing others is intelligence,
Knowing yourself is true wisdom.[2]

---

[2] Lao-Tzu, trans. Stephen Mitchell, "Chapter 33," in Tao Te Ching: A New English Version (New York, NY: HarperPerennial, 1988).

Running on Energy*

As human beings, we have a unique design — anatomically, neurologically, hormonally and chemically. While it's perfectly possible to go through life without knowing a thing about our physiological equipment (our "hardware"), a little insight into understanding normally inaccessible parts of ourselves can be helpful. Let's familiarize ourselves both intellectually and somatically, with our human design.

When it comes to our feelings, memories, reactions, thoughts, dreams, and emotions, which is where trauma, disappointment, or a tendency to feel any certain way gets lodged, we are looking primarily at our brain and nervous system. Our brain is made up of many parts and is an energy system that both uses up and emits energy. In fact, get this: although our brains weigh only two percent of our body, they use up twenty percent of our energy! It's a highly energy-consuming organ.

Our brains continually send messages throughout our body, and these messages travel along pathways made up of neurons. Each neuron is a nerve cell responsible for passing messages to the adjacent neuron along the pathway. But these neurons

---

* Although to the best of my knowledge, the information presented here is accurate, I am not a specialist in biology, chemistry, psychology or physics. Even now new discoveries may alter some of what is presented. Therefore, I invite you to use the understandings as a paradigm to help you in your own conscious evolution and elevation, rather than assuming it to be absolute scientific truth.

don't touch each other; there are gaps between one neuron and the next, which are called synapses.

It takes energy to bridge the synapse and keep the message going. Therefore, neurons are continually pumping ions into the synaptic gaps — exchanging potassium and sodium — to create an electrical energetic charge and facilitate that synaptic leap.

The human brain is made up of an estimated 100 billion neurons making a total of **100 trillion** neural connections. The total length of the nerve fiber network in the brain is approximately 500,000 km, more than the distance between the earth and the moon![3]

While we might assume that we control our thoughts and the messages being communicated throughout us, that is hardly the case. Hundreds of neural signals are continually being stimulated automatically. Indeed, a huge amount of neural pathway activity happens below our conscious awareness, and outside of our conscious control.

Some of our brain's energy is dedicated to simple housekeeping: maintaining those trillions of cells and keeping our hardware in good working order. The larger energy consumption, however, goes into managing the myriad functions our bodies continually carry out: informing, maintaining, responding, and restoring. Never are we static. Our neural network is constantly sending instructions throughout our body, building up or breaking down, in the never-ending orchestration of our physical experience.

---

[3] "Navigation System of Brain Cells Decoded," ScienceDaily (ScienceDaily, October 25, 2017), https://www.sciencedaily.com/releases/2017/10/171025105041.htm.

These pathways facilitate everything we do, like maintaining our respiration, picking up a cup, fighting off invading organisms, driving a car, preparing to mother or father a child, digesting our food, running from a threatening situation, responding to a friend's distress, re-creating a scene in our memory. Everything we experience is courtesy of our brain and nervous system.

Being designed to conserve energy where possible, our brains will minimize unnecessary output. This means once something is learned, it becomes an automatic process; unless something causes it to be redirected, it won't veer onto a different track. Hence we find ourselves doing and re-creating things the same way, without even realizing it.

When we have learned to set the table a certain way, the brain streamlines the process. Automatically we put the forks and spoons where we have learned to put them — and if someone else comes along and does it in a different way, only then will our brain take notice (and possibly offense).

This is so helpful when we are learning how to do all the millions of things that we humans can do. Learning something is literally the creating and reinforcing of neural pathways. Once done, they remain — even if later, we stop performing that activity.

The associated pathway of a defunct activity may become dormant and its energy output minimized, but the potential to reactivate it remains. For those pathways that do get regular use, their available energy activates more quickly. With enough repetition, they become automatic superhighways: constantly energized, providing ever-faster transit times.

Those processes that support our physical body's functioning, like respiration and digestion, are designed to work automatically, without our conscious participation.

However other automatic, life-preserving processes, such as our defensive system, can create experiential issues for us if their receptors trigger responses inappropriately.

We assume it's our mind that consciously perceives danger and then activates the appropriate response, but up to eighty percent of the time it's an activation sensor operating below our consciousness that picks up a threat. The sensor sends out the alert and unless consciously intercepted, initiates a fight, flight, or freeze response.

Only after our body is flooded with the fear reaction does our mind finally get the message. "Oh! I'm afraid!" leaving our brain to then figure out what the threat must be. If it's an obvious danger, the cause is clear. But if it isn't readily seen, our mind will look to justify why we are feeling this way.

For people who regularly find themselves feeling anxious or angry, that's a good clue those neural pathways of defense have become automatic superhighways. It doesn't take much to set the signals off and suddenly you are sweating, your stomach is tight, your heart racing, and your legs shaking. Alternately, you may be feeling pumped up, aggressive, and ready to take down the world!

What's going on? You may simply be driving down the street, in a meeting, or lined up in a grocery store when your system picks something up. And then, before your mind has a clue, *Boom!* The "fight, flight or freeze" train has already left the station.

This is good when we are escaping from a tiger, but not so good when our threat response has become so hyper-energized that it gets triggered even by harmless situations. Once that pathway is deeply grooved into our neural network, it doesn't bother checking in with more rational parts of our brain to make sure the reaction is warranted. It just sends out the emergency response team.

Our defense system's first priority is to keep us alive, and will continually energize the routes it has created to that end. In truly dangerous situations, instantly acting to protect, defend, or flee means we can go on to live another day. Then once the danger has passed, we are physiologically meant to be restored to a state of harmony both within ourselves and our environment.

If that restoration doesn't easily happen, or the threat level remains constantly high, the sensitivity of our receptors may have become skewed. If we have been affected by trauma, continually felt helpless in the face of danger, or remained stuck in any painful situation we couldn't integrate, our systems will become stronger in automatically re-looping our preferred emergency response. All good to keep in mind when we look at how our early influences may have affected us.

DMN — Another Way We Conserve Energy

Our brain also conserves energy when we aren't engaged in something requiring our full attention. It never actually shuts down, but when we are in a more passive moment in time, our brain reverts to re-looping old, habitual thoughts. Kicking into neural pathways where we simply **think** the same thing that we thought yesterday. And the day before, and the day before that.

Called the Default Mode Network (DMN), this programming will run habits of thought that often tend toward the critical or anxious. It harps on those things we feel aren't right or weren't done well or should be better — whether referring to ourselves, others, or something out there in the world.

Unfortunately these thoughts, like elevator music playing in the background, may affect us even though we don't necessarily like them. Because — guess what — our thoughts are entwined with, and amplified through, our emotions.

When our mind naturally reverts to remembering a time that we (or somebody else) really screwed something up, the emotions we felt back in that moment will begin running in our body. Our energy will change and point us toward a new trajectory of experience. What we think affects what we feel, physically and emotionally, which then affects what we experience. Want an example? Try this:

Close your eyes and think of something in your life that bothers you. Bring it forward mentally in whatever way you like, perhaps going to a particular situation or experience you have had. Be very present to it.

Begin to notice what your mind is saying about it. Watch the thoughts with curiosity, as though you are watching a movie. What opinions is your mind asserting on the subject?

Now notice what kind of sensations you are feeling in your body. Get specific: physical sensations, bodily feelings. What are they? Where are they? What do they feel like? Describe them to yourself.

Next, notice what kind of emotions you are feeling. Again, get specific. Consciously label your emotions. Explore them, expand them, and be fully present to them. Don't try to deny or suppress or judge, just become very aware of how you feel emotionally about this situation or experience.

Move one step further into your awareness: How would you define your energy? This is tricky. Another way to explore it is to ask yourself what you feel like doing right now. If someone were to come into the room, how might you respond to them?

Would you be open and receptive, or would you be closed and unresponsive? Would you want to do something fun with them, or would you anticipate something unpleasant or tiresome? Would you be excited to see them or wish they would go away?

In other words, are you open to what might come next into your life in a positive way, or are you feeling more negative, pessimistic, or irritable?

Consider: If that person was coming in looking forward to seeing you, but you are wishing they would turn around and walk out, how will things go? Will you snap out of your funk and be glad to see them — or might you say something snarky?

Or barky? Or maybe not say anything at all, but just sit in sulky silence?

How will that go on to affect them? Or your further interactions?

Hmmm. And all you were doing was thinking about something that isn't even happening right now.

Here's the point: Your thoughts and moods are powerful forces that carry an energy whose frequency moves through you, affecting your experience and that of others in life.

We may not know it, but we are creating it.[4]

So often our DMN-triggered thoughts revert to old voices and dictates that have been around forever. Natterings that you might not have even started, but were passed down from generation to generation, nagging, resentful, and discontented. Is it because we're just naturally grouchy old grumps? No, we just got influenced into it. But change is possible — if we want it.

Of course, even when we consciously start cultivating more satisfying, empowering thoughts, our DMN kicks in when we're not actively focusing on something. And this is such old, habitual patterning, that it easily starts up before we realize it. Once it does, suddenly here we are. Again. Mind, emotions, energy, and experience.

But there's good news: Our Default Mode Network can be distracted or turned off when we start to pay more conscious attention to our thoughts. That's what mindfulness and meditation help us do. Over time, if we dedicate enough awareness (which takes a more conscious use of our thought

---

[4] See Addendum 1 for a fuller process of tuning into your energy and gaining more conscious control over your experience.

energy, folks), we can start to create a different flavor of automatic pilot in our experience.

For now, recognize that by the time we've passed through childhood, most of us have this inner critical voice loudly broadcasting as our automatic mental default.

Neuroplasticity

Scientists used to believe that we can't change our brains, that our neural pathways are locked in for life. This is no longer the case! Scientists now realize that our brains are actually malleable and, with the proper attention, can be altered. New neural pathways can be created, with corresponding chemical, functional, and structural changes following. This is really good news and shows that each of us can transform old patterns and bring new energy and experiences forward.

The key question is — how? Well, it takes attention (i.e., conscious awareness) and desire. Without exerting some kind of influence over how we want our thoughts and messages to be transmitted, they will simply revert to the same old, same old. We have to get involved consciously to start changing our neural pathways, and create a different set point for ourselves.

Here's a very good thing to know: We can exercise synaptic pruning and direct energy away from what we don't want, by redirecting our attention into creating more enjoyable, healthy, loving, peaceful neural circuits — if we choose to.

The more energy we consciously dedicate to certain circuits, the less the brain will keep allocating to the old. Our brains, in their energy-conserving wisdom, will automatically dedicate energy toward where it is most needed, and cut back on places that are no longer getting much business.

But without engaging our attention, it won't happen. Our brains like to conserve energy too much to easily create new thoughts and habits. We have to remind ourselves, again and again, to reach for what we want to feel and be — and consciously turn away from what we don't. Otherwise our brains, oh-so-comfortable with the status quo, will keep us regurgitating all those habitual but outmoded ways of thinking, feeling and acting.

Part of the human condition is to not even know we're stuck since it's all such familiar territory. Some is so familiar that we seem to have been "born" with it. And guess what? We just might have been. But that's okay. How else will we discover what we don't want? Without experiencing what we don't want, we won't be inspired to reach for something better.

So don't berate yourself or others, and don't resist the situations that highlight something you would like to change. Instead, let them be the impetus toward a new way of experiencing and being in your life. This book will give you some ideas of how to do that.

Brain Frequencies

The last thing to understand in this brief overview of our human equipment is that brains operate within specific energetic frequencies. You may have heard of the beta or alpha or theta states; these are all different frequencies of brain waves we humans experience. Each manifests a particular awareness: a specific state of mind and range of perception. Although different parts of our brain can be operating within different frequencies at the same time, in general, our consciousness is focused in one most predominantly at any given moment.[5]

As adults in our waking hours, we mostly operate in the beta frequency range. This is outward-oriented and focused on engaging with the world: solving problems, figuring things out, planning, projecting, and brainstorming. In low- to mid-beta, this is a productive state. When the frequency moves into high beta, however, we can enter the stress zone of criticism, anxiety, and negative perceptions.

In beta, we are concerned with the business of the world, whether it's our immediate world, or the greater environment around us. Our minds are busy doing, figuring out, targeting, trying to solve problems, getting things done, feeling pressured,

---

[5] "What Is the Function of the Various Brainwaves?," Scientific American (Scientific American, December 22, 1997), https://www.scientificamerican. com/article/what-is-the-function-of-t-1997-12-22/.

remembering how things have been in the past, and worrying about how they might go in the future.

When we are falling asleep, daydreaming, or in a more meditative state of mind, our brains shift into the alpha frequency. This is a less active and more receptive state where we move beyond the beta paradigm of reality and are open to new discoveries, understandings, and solutions. Alpha accesses inspiration and creativity that beta doesn't have the bandwidth to realize.

In alpha, we can consciously begin to harness our brain's ability to bring about our own change and transformation. Many of the exercises in this book are designed to help you access this powerful state and to use it to create positive change and new possibilities for yourself.[6]

---

[6] See Addendum 2 for a full explanation of the different brain states humans experience.

Childhood Brain States

Between the ages of two to seven, children's brains are predominantly in the theta range. This is all about intensive learning — how to survive on earth. It's a state of super-absorption where everything experienced is directly translated into lessons about life.

Because childhood is the important time when humans need to learn how to survive in the world, their earliest schooling is within the family and environment where they are living. So what they see, what they hear, and what they perceive, is what they literally "write down" within their neural network as to how life is.

Since growth cannot be stopped, it's imperative a child creates this survival manual. However, children's lack of worldly experience, combined with theta's rapid absorption, means they have no ability to judge, analyze, or question the interpretations derived from their experiences.

Let's say Mother suddenly raises her voice in a panicky "Be careful!" as the child decides to mimic something they have seen her do — like carry a glass from the table to the kitchen sink.

The child's personal experience is only with plastic or some other substance, which is fine to drop on the floor or bang on the table. They don't know that glass breaks — what does "break" even mean? Or that breaking something is generally not well-received. They only know the attraction of that glass within their reach. Eager for another new experience, they seize the shiny object to bring to Mother.

But the pitch and tone of her urgent voice startle them into dropping the glass. Crash! Millions of pieces suddenly scattered everywhere! Wow! What a surprise!

Equally surprising is Mother's reaction — NOT one of delight. In fact, she gets quite angry. Or irritated. Or simply silent as she cleans up the glass and dumps it all in the garbage can.

What kinds of conclusions will that little theta brain make from this experience?

Theta mind doesn't have the capacity to analyze the situation and draw a conclusion based on all the parameters that went into it. Lesson one: They now know that glass can break. But what else do they absorb? *Breaking something is bad — and since I did it and Mom is upset, maybe I'm bad too? And if I'm bad, Mom is unhappy...with me... so I better be really careful not to break anything...*

What the child's theta brain doesn't know is that Mother hasn't gotten enough sleep lately; or is thinking about a huge project due at work; or had previously meant to move the glass away from your eager little hands, but didn't. While there are any number of situational reasons to justify her momentary reaction, all the theta mind absorbs is that their action upset Mom — and draws a very personal interpretation from it.

So many of our personal interpretations weren't really true in the greater scheme of things, yet they got absorbed and laid down in our survival manuals as the way things are. Where now, despite the advancement of our years and maturity, they may still be influencing our expectations about the world.

Of course, there are so many important lessons also being laid down — like don't cross the street when cars are coming; don't touch the hot stove; don't jump off the roof, etc., etc. All necessary learnings so we don't short-circuit our lives prematurely.

But along with all the helpful learnings are all sorts of less empowering, limiting beliefs in our capabilities. Beliefs that get buried into our developing subconscious minds, projecting an energetic braking system we take forward into our lives.

Think of a belief you have about something — something that is so evident, it's an insult to call it a belief. How about that, as a human, you don't have the capacity to fly? No one will dispute that. Sure, you can get equipment that will allow you to fly, but on your own, no way. Crash.

But a really little child doesn't know this; how would they? They see birds flying, they see leaves blowing, and they see these things called airplanes flying. Why can't they fly too?

Well, that's a lesson children need to learn early on before they can climb up to the roof and decide to take off. Somewhere along the line, they get the clear message that humans can't fly, not even Mommy or Daddy can fly. That fact is written down and underlined in their survival manual. And since I'm assuming you also don't question it, clearly, it's written in yours.

Because it was emphatically written down within your now subconscious survival manual, if you get close to the edge of a balcony or cliff, you will experience some kind of bodily reaction. Your defense system picks up the threat and immediately begins sending out messages to dramatically discourage you from getting any closer. Even before your mind registers the danger, the situation has already been assessed.

Suddenly you have butterflies in your stomach, your heartbeat speeds up, you may even feel dizzy or lightheaded. The physiological wiring in charge of keeping you safe kicks in automatically to move you away from the edge — maybe before your conscious mind even comprehends how close you are.

Recognize this: Many of the teachings in our survival manual are so ingrained that they drive our behavior automatically. Despite all the stock we put into our conscious mind's ability to assess, make choices, and act, this is only part of how we interact with life. Our conscious mind isn't even that big a part of us — although we tend to ascribe everything we believe we are to it.

Below that relatively small portion of our human operating system is a whole realm of unknown and unconscious triggers, many derived directly from our earliest experiences and assumptions. These silent influences continually direct neurological, chemical, and hormonal signals to be sent throughout our bodies. They use our energy and affect our physical sensations, emotions, thoughts, actions, and reactions.

As we go further into this book, keep in mind that this is part of our human design. We all are affected by unconscious but still potent belief interpretations, continuing to exert powerful influences over our life experiences. While many of them have stood us in good stead, others are no longer helpful, keeping us stuck in repetitive or unhelpful patterns.

You may recognize some painful or limiting beliefs still alive within yourself. You may label parts of your past — certain experiences, certain people's actions, or even parts of yourself — as having been wrong.

Recognize your assessment, but don't believe in it too strongly. Decide you are ready to discover if there is a deeper right hiding beneath some of your assumptions of wrong. This is the meaning of transformation. When we can turn what seemed to be a wrong into a right, we become channels of grace for the world. We become truly free.

What's Your State of Mind?

Try on this thought: *What our eyes perceive as solid is actually a vibrating, morphing, continually coming together and moving apart of both waves and particles. Within a flash, our senses interpret and hold a particular picture of what we think of as "reality," but in another dimension, is anything but static. Although our thought-form will continue to hold "reality" in a particular fixed pattern for us (until we look in a different way), there are other potentials ever ready to be perceived.*

Our beta brains, focused on how to negotiate life in the outer world, operate almost exclusively through interpretations/ assumptions made from the past. Many of these assumptions were developed during our theta years — when our physical senses and emotions interpreted "reality" from our early experiences. Even though our environment and those in it are now vastly different, beta mind still uses this past assumption of reality in its projections/decisions about the future, to determine how we should show up in the world.

There is nothing inherently wrong with this. As long as our beta version of reality keeps us functional and not harming ourselves or others, it's the practical frequency through which we feed ourselves, keep the roof over our heads, perform assigned tasks, complete exams, and drive safely on the roads.

It's not, however, our most creative, evolutionary state. Often it keeps us stuck in a less satisfying version of reality based on our past, rather than envisioning ever-deeper, more beneficial potentials for ourselves and our world. Just keep that in mind as you continue through this book.

Energy and Matter: Two Sides of the Same Coin

Quantum physicists have discovered that everything — EVERYTHING! — is a manifestation of energy. $E = mc^2$ is physicist Albert Einstein's theory of special relativity that basically says mass (matter) and energy are interchangeable — different forms of the same thing. Something that we perceive as solid — like the chair you are sitting in — is actually made up of ever-moving, vibrating, energy.

Energy has different wavelengths, from very long to very short, from high amplitude to low amplitude. Now our physical senses can see a chair, but they can't see a gamma-ray. It exists, both as a mass as well as energy, but our bodies don't have the equipment to perceive it. We come with sensory attunement only to matter vibrating within a particular band of frequencies. We are oblivious to manifestations vibrating outside those frequencies and must rely on other instruments to perceive, define, and give meaning to.

What about thoughts? They travel through neural pathways, which require energy to be transmitted. And since energy is also mass, a thought is both an energy and a "thing," a substance.[7]

---

[7] "What Actually Is a Thought? and How Is Information Physical?," Psychology Today (Sussex Publishers), accessed July 26, 2022, https://www.psychologytoday.com/ca/blog/finding-purpose/201902/what-actually-is-thought-and-how-is-information-physical.

We can't actually perceive our thoughts through our five externally oriented senses, so we don't give them much credit as a substance. But a thought of love has a very different "feel" than a thought of hate. We may not be able to see, touch, hear, smell, or taste our thoughts, but their energy affects us — and others.

When we think a thought, we are projecting energy/mass out into the world. But we're getting ahead of ourselves: first, let's look at the manifestation we know of as "us," or human beings.

Who are you? Are you this body? This body that changes, morphs, and goes through a whole lifetime of experiences, thoughts, actions, etc.? Is that the extent of you? Because of our human design, this is what seems to be true and what our experiences reinforce us to believe.

The design of this "me" in this physical human body, and the progression of our brain's development, ensures we are educated into believing what our senses tell us about reality. Since we experience our lives from within a physical structure that appears separate and different than everything else, we believe ourselves to be separate. We come to trust that the boundary of reality is what we can see, hear, taste, touch, and smell. Anything we cannot perceive through our senses is highly suspect.

Our brains, with their biological senses, are like a computer program — designed to interpret only a particular segment of all the energetic frequencies surrounding us. Our eyes, ears, nose, tongue, and skin's surface can only register experiences within a particular range of energetic frequencies. This is simply the way we are designed.

We are energy in matter, experiencing a physically separate evolution we call our life, within the time/space-bound environment we call earth.

But just exactly WHAT or WHO is experiencing our life? Our earth? Is it simply a brain function? A nervous system function? A bunch of electrical impulses (also energy) that are running us and could be measured and taken apart in a science lab?

Or is there something beyond our wiring, something mysterious, something that makes us more than just our current physiological reality as manifested within this human energetic blueprint?

Exploring Our Ever-Shifting Reality

When it comes to the physical manifestations of energy, it's pretty hard to deny our separateness. I am me and you are you and we are clearly different! But what causes us to experience this differentiation?

It seems to be our physiological equipment — especially our brain and nervous system — that translates the various energies in and around us and gives rise to the this's and that's of our world. How do we perceive reality through our nervous system? Let's do some exploring.

Tuning Into Your Nervous System

Sit quietly, away from distractions. Don't do this if you are driving, or anywhere/time when you need to be alert to the external world.

Think of a stressful situation you are currently dealing with in your life. Close your eyes and turn your attention inside, into your body.
What do you notice?
Where do you notice things?
What kind of physical sensations do you feel?
How do you experience the sensations?
What do they feel like? Get specific.

Explore your sensations further.
Describe the sensations to yourself in more detail.
Their quality. Density. Whether they stay static or change.

Do they remain in one spot or radiate? Move around? Connect to other parts of your body, or remain separate?

Don't try and change anything, simply tune in and observe whatever physical sensations you experience when you think of this stressful situation.

Now: Tune into any emotions you may be feeling.

Very likely, these are quite present to you; maybe even easier to identify than the physical sensations.

As you name your emotions, ask yourself, "What is the sensation of this particular emotion within my body?"

Be an observant detective of whatever is happening within you. Keep your eyes closed and simply remain focused on your inner experience.

Don't try to change anything, just be present to whatever is happening inside you as you consider this stressful situation.

Now — as you remain present and aware of whatever is happening within you, continue to observe and describe to yourself what you are experiencing. Name your sensations. Describe them to yourself and continue to feel them without trying to change or suppress them. Simply be present, open, and acknowledging of them, continually aware of and following them within yourself.

Next, notice whether you are experiencing any reaction not only to the situation, but perhaps to your own physical, emotional reaction itself.

What is happening within your physical chemistry? Your neurology? Continue to remain very observant.

Notice what happens within you, the cycle you go through when you feel under this particular stress.

Again, don't try and change anything, simply observe and allow these processes within you to happen. Simply be with yourself and your experience.

As you remain very present to your inner experiences — sensations, emotions, thoughts — and continue to observe them without judging or trying to change them, ask yourself these questions:

How safe do I feel right now?

How comfortable am I in my body right now?

How connected or close do I feel to other people, including those who might be part of the situation, right now?

How would I describe my energy right now?

Don't judge what you observe or feel, as you consider those questions. They are simply here to help you understand what happens in your personal stress cycle, when your nervous system gets activated.

You may notice a desire to move or shift a part of your body; go ahead and let your body do anything it wants to do, such as shift or stretch or shake or vibrate. Remain keenly present to every aspect of your body's movements.

Follow any changes that occur in your body as a result of your movements.

Remain present and aware of whatever is happening within you.

Now see if you can let the image of the situation, or whatever has been causing you stress, to fade away a bit. Remain very present to your inner experience as you remember that this isn't actually happening anywhere other than in your body/mind. Bring yourself back to the here and now, to sitting in your chair, to this moment where there is no need for you to take any action or solve any problems, even as you continue to focus on whatever is going on within you.

Continue to notice your physical sensations, your emotions, and any thoughts that are running through your mind. Don't buy into them, but don't resist them either. You simply want to be fully present to whatever is happening inside, watching without any resistance.

Notice how things may be shifting. Perhaps the sense of danger or anger or tightness or constriction begins to lessen a bit. Remember — you are simply sitting here, no one is threatening or disturbing you in actuality. It's all been an inner journey and now you are letting it go.

Take a few deep breaths and let them out slowly, slowly. Open your eyes and see if you can find something soothing or enjoyable to look at. Notice any further internal loosening or relaxing that may be taking place.

Ask yourself: Have I fully let go of any of the stressful feelings I conjured up? How connected to other people and the world around me do I now feel?

The little process we just did was to explore the automatic wiring system all us humans have and to discover how your energy never ceases, even when sitting still. Whether you are actually in a threatening, stressful situation or just thinking about it, your brain and body are in concert, automatically reacting. Once that activation happens, you experience a whole cascade of physiological, chemical, neurological, and even hormonal processes, affecting your body, mind, emotions, all of which is part of your energy field.

As you thought of the stressful situation, you likely noticed tightening or constriction in your body — maybe your stomach, chest, shoulders, neck, or head. You may have experienced some unpleasant emotions — fear, anger, panic, frustration. And your mind was probably telling you in no uncertain terms all the things wrong with this situation.

Here are some questions to ask yourself, as you become more aware of your personal nervous system and the energy you emanate:

How would you describe your energy when you were in that moment?

What kind of effect might that energy have on how you feel about yourself, your life, and others in that moment?

What kind of an effect would that energy have on your body, as it runs through you?

Just think about it.

When you go into an automatic stress reaction, there is lots of interesting physiological activity. For our purposes, you want to begin making conscious what has previously been below your awareness. To consciously feel and observe what is happening on the different levels of your body, mind, emotions, and energy whenever you get activated.

The three main reactions of the stress-activated nervous system are fight, flight, and freeze. Thinking back to what you noticed within yourself; can you identify which of those states you felt yourself to be in?

Fight is an aggressive, angry, hot sense where you feel people/ situations are against you and you must rise up to fight. Flight is more like the prey animal suddenly bursting into motion to escape the lion bearing down on them — wanting to get the hell out of Dodge. Freeze is the deer frozen in the headlights, so overcome with fear that it cannot even speak, think, or move.

When we are in the grips of a stress or defensive response, we truly feel alone and there is no sense of safety, relaxation, or community (except with those sharing our experience in the same way). It's an alienating state that we aren't meant to stay in very long, as basically it uses all our resources — our energy — to mount a defense against whatever is threatening us so we can escape.

Once the threat is over, our optimal human blueprint wiring is to return to a state of relaxation, rejuvenation, reconnection, and restoration. In that state you feel relaxed and connected with others, your body can repair, rest, and restore, and you return to activities that interest or inspire you. Just now you may have witnessed yourself go through the whole cycle, observing your bodily sensations, emotions, and thoughts running their course and eventually returning to feeling relaxed and at ease.

If you did return to a state of well-being, that's great; you have a healthy, automatic ability to return to a state of rest, relaxation, community, and safety. But if you remained on alert even after recognizing there was no threat, then likely you have developed some robust superhighways into the fight/flight/freeze response and don't easily feel safe or at ease in the world.

That's okay — it's good simply to realize this. It doesn't mean you are doomed to perpetual anxiety or rage, just that you aren't realizing potentials alive, but still untapped, within. There is some retuning you are ripe to do to create a more satisfying, enjoyable life experience.

Are you getting a sense of the ever-changing inner landscape within your body, your emotions, and your mind? And are you getting a sense of a larger consciousness you can access that transcends the moment-to-moment experience?

Your nervous system's wiring isn't a bad thing — after all, it's kept you alive. But as long as it's running the show without a realistic differentiation of what is truly threatening, it will keep shooting off old, habitual reactions where you are like a pinball bouncing from one crisis to another.

Getting to know yourself and your reactions is the first step in actively guiding your neural pathways into more satisfying, benevolent directions. Coming to discern and direct your larger authority over automatic reactions is the practice of self-mastery.

Keep these aspects of your human blueprint and wiring — your hardware, software, and potentials of greater awareness — in the back of your mind as we go forward and explore the coming into being of a human — the wondrous, mysterious expression of YOU.

PART II
Conception

Where Did You Come From?

When my first child was conceived, getting pregnant was the furthest thought from my mind. My boyfriend and I had gone through three exciting but also turbulent on-again/off-again years. At the moment we were sort of back on again — but he wasn't making any noises about the future.

I was twenty-eight, living in New York City, haphazardly pursuing a career as an opera/musical theater singer. This was great but also required a day job to pay the rent. After a few less-than-satisfying positions, I was finally in a job that was flexible, with a kind and supportive boss.

Life was fun! I performed here and there, went to auditions, went to work, and was once again connected to Dennis — whom I deeply cared about, even as we kept going back and forth in the gradual growth of our relationship.

One night we had gone out for dinner and returned to his apartment. The intimacy was sweet and afterward, suddenly, I had a flash of knowing — spontaneous, without any kind of emotion — that someone was coming in. Not like coming in through the front door, but like — coming IN, coming in. A new... awareness. A new presence. I had a sudden flash of insight that we had conceived a...

But that was ridiculous! Dennis had fertility issues and doctors had told him the chances of getting someone pregnant the old-fashioned way were slim to none. Because this flash had been more like a download of impersonal information without any feeling behind it, I simply forgot about it.

Fast-forward six or seven weeks. I was feeling strange. Tired and hungry all the time, kind of bloated, just a little off. One Saturday night I was singing a duet with a friend at a performance gathering in lower Manhattan. Afterward there was wine and food, but I just didn't feel like having anything.

And suddenly the thought "could I be *pregnant?*" hit me. KABOOM! I made the mental calculation to my last period — just when had it been? I couldn't even remember, it was so long ago.

This time, when the knowing thought registered, there were plenty of feelings, and they weren't good ones. More like a sinking panic on the way to sheer terror. Oh, shit.

I went home and barely slept until I could go to the pharmacy and get a home pregnancy test — which confirmed what I already knew. I was pregnant.

For those of you who have longed to get pregnant, who have agonized over trying to conceive, it might be a bitter blow to hear a story like that — indeed later, I also would struggle through miscarriages and years of infertility. But this pregnancy was totally, completely unexpected, coming out of left field, a sudden sharp turn off a slowly meandering path.

Pregnancy happens, who really knows how. Whether mentally or financially ready, whether in a stable relationship or not, somehow the moment lines up. Regardless of how we react to the result, we have entered into the realm of mystery: The creation of something out of nothing, the manifestation of a new and unique human being.

How does a new person come into the world? While fairy tales portray it done through a loving relationship ready and waiting to bring forth a child, that's hardly standard. How many babies are conceived and brought into the world through less "appropriate" circumstances? And yet — we come! Even when we aren't always wanted or able to be cared for by the parents whose bodies give us the entrance. Something happens, and the readying energy comes on in.

See if you can feel this for yourself. YOU were already an energy, a vibration, a consciousness even, an unseen presence ready to be manifest. Even before you began to become YOU, there was a power, a potential gathering of energy, of forces readying to move into the realm of SOME THING; and when the opportunity came, when the energy was ignited and met with a human spark, YOU began.

The Calling of the Creative Force

Sit quietly and think of a time when something truly and powerfully life-altering came forward; something that you hadn't ever imagined happening.

Perhaps meeting someone who went on to be important to you.

Perhaps discovering a place that you felt a strong connection to.

Perhaps hearing a story that gave you goosebumps.

Perhaps discovering something in your education or job or seemingly unexpected happenstance that proved to be a pivotal moment in your life's path.

Think back; take your time and allow something to come forward. There may be many moments. Pick one you would like to explore.

Now — holding this moment in your mind, close your eyes. Turn your attention inward and travel back in your mind's eye to that experience. Allow yourself to see it fully.

Where were you? See the place.
Look around it. Fill it out.

What colors do you notice? Are you revisiting in more muted tones, or do you notice anything vibrant? See if you can fill out the colors more clearly. The color of the furniture or what you were wearing. The details of what was around you, whether small or large.

How about location — are you outside? Inside?

What are you doing? If you are sitting, what are you sitting on? If standing or walking or running or doing whatever you were doing, focus in on that. Feel it — the sensations in your body or against your body.

What sounds might have been heard? Cars or footsteps or muted conversations or music... Tune into the sounds of the experience, as they were happening in the moment.

Are you with someone? Notice where they are in this moment. What are they doing? Become present to their participation in this experience, in however small a way.

Go back further in your mind's eye to all the preceding experiences, actions, or decisions that brought you to this pivotal moment, this pivotal meeting, this pivotal juncture in your life.

Notice all the things that had to happen for this moment to have come about. All the different paths that could have prevented you from being here, all the choices you had to make in order to meet this particular moment of destiny.

Look deeply into the moment itself. What happens?

Live the moment, the meeting, the experience. Play it out once again in your mind's eye.

Do you have any inkling of what this moment will mean in your life?

Perhaps yes, and perhaps no, it's okay either way. Just become very aware of how potent that moment, that experience, that meeting, has been to you — and yet how randomly it may have seemed to occur.

Notice all that this moment began to usher forward into your life. Move forward in your mind's eye and see the future it brought to you begin to unfold.

Be aware of your emotions as you start to unpack the full destiny of that experience, of that person, of that future you perhaps had never even imagined, as it slowly but surely opened up and blossomed in your life.

Notice whatever you might be feeling. Often our experiences can seem to be mixed blessings — lots of good, but also a fair portion of pain or unpleasantness.

We rarely have anything that's pure bliss, but that's not really to be expected when living in these forever-changing human bodies, in this forever-changing external world.

We do our best growing within a variable spectrum of experiencing, so even if you notice portions of this future that didn't work out, that met an unhappy end or that veered onto a totally different track, that's okay.

Rather than focus on how things didn't work out, simply appreciate the parts of the journey where you clearly see how you did benefit, how you did grow, and how you discovered things about yourself that have remained important and meaningful.

And if you find yourself going down a painful cul-de-sac of feelings, breathe a little more deeply. Consciously and gently create a little more space within your body, within your psyche, to accommodate all the different facets that have made up your great life adventure — your hero's journey — without negating any of them.

You might even recognize how those parts that didn't work out opened a window for something important and powerful to come forward.

See if you discover the path that, while meandering, has also been one of meaning and purpose through the many adventures and moments of your life.

Allow yourself to feel this deeper course, this deeper drawing of your own destiny or passage.

Consider that no matter how random life may seem, you are part of something vaster than what your mind alone may notice. Just sit with this for a few moments.

In your own time, you can open your eyes.

Look at something close to you.

See it in its wholeness — even if it's just a piece of furniture or a dust mote in the air.

See its distinct nature, its beingness.

It, too, has had its own journey and will continue its journey of change, no matter how minor its manifested role might be in your life.

There is so much around us all the time. So many things, so many sensory experiences, and so many possibilities we could follow. Emerging from all the noisy distractions clamoring for attention — the manifested stuffing of the world, the forever ticking moments of time, the infinite places where we could have been, the situations we could have encountered, the people we could have met — do the moments of our lives unfold.

How these random moments add up is an equation we can never fully understand, and yet — there is a creative principle, a force that draws us always forward, always to the new, always ready and waiting underneath all our pregnant pauses. We are forever conceiving or gestating or delivering. Ourselves.

Confirmation

When the fact of my pregnancy was confirmed, it was like stepping into space. My life as I knew it, was in abeyance. What would come next was completely unknown.

I called Dennis, saying we needed to have a talk. We met at a diner nearby, and he arrived with a dubious look on his face. In the past, these "talks" usually meant a last-chance opportunity to make a bid for a deeper relationship. Learning that I was pregnant would have been the last thing he expected, and I didn't have a clue what his reaction might be.

Early on in our dating, he told me that having a family (i.e., children) was almost more important to him than having a wife. That took me aback (what could be more family than a wife?) but I rationalized that his previous, childless marriage lay behind his statement.

Overall, it had been quite convenient to date someone who couldn't get me pregnant; we had become lackadaisical in doing anything to avoid that possibility. But now here it was, the unthinkable had happened — in the middle of a relationship that was familiar, comfortable, but still completely uncommitted.

Dennis listened to me blurt out the news. There was a moment of silence, shock in his eyes, and then — he transformed. Although he was still sitting across the table with the same cup of coffee, he nano-seconded forward into a whole new future.

His first words were: "Do you want to have a real wedding, or should we just elope?"

Wait a minute... I wasn't even sure I wanted to be with this guy who had, more than once, relegated me to a back seat in his life, who had made it clear, more than once, that while he cared for me, he wasn't interested in taking it any further. And now, in this single instant, he was suggesting — no, radiating — that this baby was meant to be, that our relationship was meant to be, and that our future as a family was firmly settled.

I don't remember what I said. It certainly wasn't a wholehearted "YES!" but more like a squeaky, "Well, maybe." I went back to my apartment with my head spinning. What to do... part of me yearned to be swept along into his enthusiasm and confidence, while another part of me felt anything but.

This confusion remained, even as I called my parents and told them we were engaged. Even as we moved forward with wedding plans. Even as I gagged my way through more than one congratulatory dinner.

Being engaged and planning a wedding is usually the main event, but when you are also pregnant, the stage is shared. My own hesitant uncertainty, even as I kept walking forward, made the whole first part of my pregnancy more like an alternate reality I had suddenly become stuck in — instead of one I had mindfully determined for myself.

Pregnant — what does that word mean to you? We think of its usage in more ways than one: from the purely biological meaning of growing a new life, to the more metaphorical aspects, like "a pregnant pause." It speaks of a length of time in which something already exists, but hasn't been revealed. Full of meaning. Potential. Significant. Suggestive.

When we think of our own beginnings, consider that the sudden suggestion of us came in the middle of full lives our parents were already living. Complicated, practical, still figuring it out, surviving-in-the-outer-world lives. No matter how eagerly anticipated or how totally inconvenient our pregnancy was, our parents had complete existences of their own, into which the unknown us inserted itself.

Have you ever seen pictures of your parents before you were born? Or before you were even a thought on the horizon? Have you ever seen them as children, teenagers, or young adults? Perhaps you are a child who came later in their lives, behind other siblings. Perhaps you never even thought of them as having an existence before you.

See if you can find or remember pictures of them before they became parents. Before there was you.

Look at their faces in the pictures. What do you see?

It can be something to think about: How much did our parents really know about themselves, about life, about their own potential, when we were born to them? For those of us who were given up by a parent or parents, we know even less, just that they didn't have the capacity to care for us, that they chose to release us to a hopefully better life than they felt able to provide.

It might be helpful to remember that parents, just like us, continue to evolve. An act taken in a moment of frustration or when feeling overwhelmed, an unconscious repetition of pain previously inflicted upon them, may have become a memory set in concrete for you; a "reality" you continue to apply.

How many of us take on a belief about our parents based on an action done or words spoken — often at their own worst moments?

Meeting Your Parents

Sit quietly and close your eyes. Turn your attention inward, into your body. Allow yourself to become aware of any sensations you may be experiencing.

Any physical sensations.
Any emotions.

Remain very open and present to whatever is coming forward in a receptive, even welcoming, attitude.

If your mind is noisy, be present to it also, but without buying into the thoughts. Remember, the beta brain is all about doing — solving problems, going back over so-called mistakes, trying to find better ways to do things… all in the outer world.

But now we are deliberately turning away from this outer world and consciously shifting our focus and brain waves into a kind of inner awareness: inner perceptions of the vast, complex world always alive and active within us.

So become more and more focused on your sensations, on what you are perceiving within yourself.

Notice the emotions you may be experiencing.
Notice the thoughts that may come forward.
Notice what your thoughts are saying.

Be present, but don't identify yourself with your thoughts. It's so easy for us to think our thoughts are "us," that they are what makes us who and what we are — but that's not true. Our thoughts are simply energy that we can reinforce and make more solid, or let flow along without giving any further emphasis.

As you continue to simply observe and focus your conscious-ness on whatever is happening within yourself right now, invite your breath to slow down a bit. Invite the inhales to come a little deeper into your body.

Observe, invite, and allow the breath in more deeply without any force or insistence.

Step back from trying to DO anything; simply invite, observe, and follow. Spend a few minutes just inviting the breath in more deeply, and following what happens.

Now — in your mind's eye, invite a memory of your parents — either your mother or father or both — to come forward.

Invite them with the intention of understanding something you hadn't previously been aware of. Something you misunderstood or misinterpreted or just didn't know. About them.

Take your time here. If you feel some trepidation about this, ask that it be something small, something easy, something you are completely ready to see and now understand from a place of safety and kindness.

If that feels impossible, if your memories and feelings of a parent are too much to even approach, then be kind to yourself and only do what feels appropriate right now. Back off whenever you have gone far enough.

Continue to let your breathing be slow and gentle, again no forcing of anything, no "doing." You are simply receptive and open, allowing memories to come forward in a new light. In a new understanding. In discovering something you have been seeking for a long time, and are now ready to experience in the fullness of a more expansive truth.

As a child, you had a limited perspective. Your understanding of the world, of humans, of the immensity of the human experience, was but an infant's grasp. So many things we little ones misunderstood, so many things we misinterpreted, so many things were beyond our mind's ability to comprehend in a fuller way.

There is no shame in this, it's simply part of our journey. Yet how often do we get stuck in a memory that only contained the partial story, that couldn't encompass the larger picture, the ever-changing, ever-dissolving and rebuilding of reality?

Look carefully and closely at your parent. Look into their eyes. Notice their expression.
Notice things about them you have never noticed before.
What are they concerned about in this moment?
What are the burdens that could be weighing them down?
What are the cares and concerns they are trying to figure out?
What are the dreams and desires, the deeper purpose they are trying to fulfill for themselves in the world?

As you continue to look at them, perhaps you begin to feel what might have been true for them at that moment.

If you find yourself thinking the same thoughts about them that you have always thought, deliberately dis-engage from those thoughts; keep yourself open.

What would it feel like to see a new aspect or perspective of them?

There is likely much more to them than you have realized before, so remain present and curious.

And remain kind — to them, and to yourself.

Perhaps breathe consciously into your heart area, as you remain present.

If you notice even the smallest thing about them in a new way, be open to it — and to your inner sensations and feelings.

It can be a shock to see someone we thought we knew in a new light; it can feel discombobulating, as though the reality you have always believed in is suddenly dissolving.

That's okay. Go ahead and let it dissolve, let the sands shift. Stay present to whatever you are experiencing, without shutting anything down. Simply allow a new reality to come forward, a new understanding about your parent(s).

Stay present to your emotions. Perhaps you are feeling very uncomfortable, in pain, or not wanting to stay with this. Or perhaps you are feeling a lightness and a new sense of freedom.

Whatever you are feeling, stay present and allow things to shift and move as they flow.

You are exploring a new possibility. Allow it to take whatever shape it wants.

Be gentle and kind to yourself, to all parts of this experience right now.

When you feel you have reached a conclusion — or simply must move along and return to the outer world — try to sit for another minute and allow whatever you have learned or seen to remain present a bit longer. Often, we need to simply be quiet for a minute to allow a new integration within us.

This process will, of course, continue — and it's helpful if you can return to this new awareness again and again over the next few days and weeks, further aligning its new truth into your experience.

Creative Drawing, Dreaming, Writing

For many of us, giving a new understanding some creative expression can be a powerful way to further integrate our evolution and growth. Perhaps you would like to draw or dance an expression of what you have experienced. Perhaps you would like to write about it.

The more you can expand the fullness of this new understanding in different ways, the more it will become alive in you. These changes will ripple further out within you, and eventually into your ongoing experience. Let your imagination, your creativity, even the movement of your body, enliven whatever you have discovered.

Energize your new understanding and give it space to expand. Like pregnancy itself, allow the new potential you have discovered to morph and grow roots. To expand beyond your old, cramped perceptions into something spacious and light.

Allow this expansiveness its full expression — through writing, dancing, music, art, or in whatever way you are moved to manifest — and continue to fill out the pictures and memories you have of your parent or parents.

They were so much more than you realized, their existence so much fuller, more complicated.

While we may have fixed our parents in our minds like a bug to a board, perhaps you now have a sense of their own continual processing and changing. Of other possibilities within them, still available for you.

A New Relation to Time and Space

"When the energy of Heaven meets the energy of earth,
Birth and death appear.
Between birth and death,
Life appears." [8]

Pregnancy engenders a new experience of time and space. We adults have already learned a lot about time, about how long something takes. Like finishing a school year. Getting your first driver's license. Completing an apprenticeship. Obtaining a degree. Building a house. Baking a loaf of bread.

So much of our lives revolve around the length of time it takes to bring a goal or idea to fruition.

Our beta brains connect a meaningful use of time, with **doing**. We commit ourselves to some thing — a project, recipe, program, skill — that requires time and energy. If we stay the course, we will see a result, whether it be a baked cake or a Ph.D.

---

[8] Bright-Fey, J. "Chapter 50." Essay. In The Whole Heart of the Tao: The Complete Teachings from the Oral Tradition of Lao-Tzu, Birmingham, AL; Crane Hill Publishers, 2006

But pregnancy brings forth a different connection to doing and time. Oh, we had to do something all right, and often without any intention of this outcome! Other times the intention has become so upfront and center, that we are working doggedly towards the goal of getting pregnant above all else.

But regardless of how it is set into motion, once pregnancy happens, we enter into a new dimension where instead of us using time, time is using us. Even though there is nothing for us to do, this human is being developed through time. It takes about forty weeks before the concept of us manifests into a fully formed baby, ready to emerge into the world.

When we think about space, often we are really thinking about all the objects that take up space. We look around and see things — the chair, the dishes in the sink, the computer, the food in the fridge.

Our eyes are drawn to the things around us, followed by the thoughts that those things inspire. Clean up the kitchen. Get that report done. Service the car, put ink in the printer, set the table, replace that lightbulb, organize the taxes, whatever.

We mostly focus on the forms around us and what they represent. We forget that before, after, and surrounding all the "things" of our lives, is space.

The one form or thing we are most connected to, in terms of taking up space, is our own body. Just how do you relate to yourself as being a body? This mass with legs, arms, head, mouth that talks, ears that hear, eyes that see, mind that thinks.

Are you aware of your bone structure, your internal organs? Or the many systems constantly at work within? Do you have a visceral sense of the trillions of cells continually regenerating and recreating themselves? Do you have any idea of what goes into keeping you alive, so you can have this physical experience on earth?

Not likely. Mostly we move through life with little awareness of the inner workings of our bodies, and instead treat them more like a piece of equipment we expect to function adequately. We only pay much attention when some part starts going *ker-thunk*.

But with pregnancy — suddenly the status quo of living in our bodies is changed. The very space we take up becomes altered as organs shift around, uteruses expand, breasts enlarge, bellies protrude. We come to realize our space, the most personal space we know, is suddenly being shared.

Familiar and automatic functions of our bodies — eating, digesting, sleeping, peeing — change, along with the alteration of our space. And then — movement! Kicks and bumps and lumps. There is something alive in here: something that is in us, but isn't us.

Just where did it come from? Nowhere. And yet — it is taking up more and more space.

With the start of pregnancy, the energetic essence of us begins to take physical form. Pregnant parents become the vehicle necessary to bring the ethereal "nothing" of our pure potential, into the something of us as a physical being.

The idea that we already were, that there was an existence of an "us" that preceded that of our physical form, is something we might have considered but have trouble relating to.

And yet — what were we before we began to come into this beingness? How did we emerge with our individual personalities, gifts- and deficits-in-waiting? Could it be that there was an energetic "me" prior to conception that fit itself seamlessly into the genetic blueprint of the combined egg and sperm?

Could it be we are energetic essences already in existence, anticipating this earthly life?

Conception and pregnancy are when we become embodied, literally, by energies winnowed out of infinite possibilities. Drawn together out of the vast, unexplainable soup of potential, comes the etheric, energetic, cosmic whomever we will become. And through a single very human action, a man and woman become the makers and means of this brand-new trajectory of expression, streaming in from the infinite. Ourselves.

Dreaming of a Being

After we hosted a small, traditional wedding, Dennis and I began to settle into not just married life, but that of soon-to-be parents.

Along with my cat Cleo, I'd moved into Dennis' apartment — where previously I'd only ever kept a toothbrush and hairdryer. I was still a tentative newlywed, comfortable in some areas but tiptoeing my way in others. We'd made this drastic sea change so quickly, I wasn't fully up to speed with it; it still felt unreal.

My body was showing clear signs of what was growing inside. The nausea and tiredness of the first few months had passed, and there came the day when I began to feel the fluttering of this human being growing inside me.

Early on, I decided this baby was a boy. Partly because I wanted to be okay with having a son. I knew nothing of little boys, except being daunted by the huge energy that seemed to explode from their small bodies. Dennis was the last male in his family to carry the family name, so feeling a bit like the queen having to provide that male heir, I ignored the distinct possibility that this baby could be anything other than a boy.

In those days, parents weren't learning the sex of the baby so freely as they do today. That required an amniocentesis, a somewhat risky procedure recommended only for mothers over the age of thirty-five. For me at twenty-eight, this wasn't going to happen; so I continued my projection that we were having a boy, and voiced it whenever the subject came up.

Shopping for the baby, I even bought a few blue things — reinforcing my complete willingness to have a boy. I remained vigilant in denying the slightest suggestion that there could be a daughter growing inside.

In the middle of my pregnancy, I had a series of dreams. In them, my baby was born and we were together. There wasn't a clear distinction of their sex, but there was a sense of being deeply connected. Strangely, although it felt totally wonderful in that dream/reality, the baby alternated between being a human baby, and Cleo, my beloved feline companion.

Although my waking hours weren't so clear, in the deeper brain waves of dreaming, there was a sense of complete connection and knowing of this presence. It was a timeless, spacious experience of pure love.

I would awaken in the middle of the night feeling peaceful, an oasis during those confusing and sometimes turbulent days. Although I would talk about a boy and continue to try and relate to this baby as being a particular sex, the deeper connection went beyond gender.

Pregnancy, regardless of how the parents feel about it in the outer world, is a portal. It allows us glimpses beyond the veil of our earth-focused reality into the realms of space and energy. A place where we partner in the most fundamental creation of all: universal energy concentrated into a human being.

Discovering Space

Can you imagine yourself before coming into this world? As pure energy or consciousness or soul, or whatever concept you could imagine. This is difficult for our beta brains — so let's be adventurous and invite our alpha minds forward. Here is where we can explore wider possibilities than what the beta can accommodate, and open ourselves to something new.

Try this: Close your eyes and take some time to turn your attention away from worldly concerns and thoughts. Sometimes the easiest way to do this is to focus on your breath.

First, just become aware of your breath.
If possible, breathe in and out only through your nose.

Notice how you are breathing.
Follow the inhale. Follow the exhale.
Keep watching. Notice what the rhythm of your breath is like.
Notice where the breath goes in your body.

Simply observe without trying to change or alter anything.
Now, as you continue to feel or watch the inhale, begin to count its length; then follow and begin to count the length of your exhale.
Repeat.
Keep your attention on your breath, without trying to "do" anything, but simply becoming absorbed in the counting of your inhale, the counting of your exhale.

Continue focusing on your breathing and counting for at least ten cycles.

Now, still attentive to your breathing, release the need to count the lengths and instead become more focused on the breath itself.
What is coming in? What is going out?
See if you can feel the quality of your breath. In. Out.
What is the substance of your breath?
Does it have a substance?
How would you describe it?
Explore your breath even more deeply.
Allow yourself to keep following and exploring just what the breath is.

How would you describe breath to someone else?

Where does your breath come from? Where does it go? Begin to get a sense of the space of your breath, both inside and out. Keep your focus, your exploration, on your breath.

If you find yourself getting distracted by other things (noises, thoughts), then return your attention to your breath. You may find this is hard work — surprisingly, this type of focus requires a great deal of active attention to maintain — so don't be surprised if you keep wandering off.

When you notice you have wandered, just return to your breath without setting up an inner dialogue about it.
Just return to your breath.

Eventually, start to focus on the experience of breath as space.
The space of breath.
Inside your body.
Outside your body.
Notice that breath isn't really a thing at all; it's more like space-in-action.
Space moving in. Space moving out.

Notice that space doesn't change, whether it's inside or outside of your body.
Notice that this space is all around you.
That it stretches out. And out.
That it goes beyond the room or place you are sitting in. That it goes beyond your immediate surroundings. Beyond your town or city or county or state. Beyond your country. That this space covers oceans and mountains.

Perhaps you will get a sense of this space, this air, this breath, as covering our entire planet. That our planet itself is breathing space, that all the inhabitants of the planet, whether humans, animals, trees, oceans, mountains, are breathing. In. Out.

Perhaps you can consider that all the doings on the planet — all the human actions and interactions, from love-making to wars — take place against this backdrop of breath.
Of space.
Of space breathing.
Of space being breathed.
Something we do automatically without thinking about it. Something that is happening continually, and we aren't even aware of it.
Automatic, unconscious, our breath goes beyond time.

This breath stretches out forever in terms of our physical experience of it.
We are nurtured and held and breathed by this space, this breath.

It maintains our life, holds us, is the cradle of our experiences and the neutral backdrop behind our disappointments and triumphs.

Breath. Space. It simply IS.

See if you can feel yourself as simply Being Space.

Beyond your body, beyond your thoughts, beyond your achievements and triumphs, beyond your regrets and failures. Just be space. Just be your breath. Just be present.

In your own time, you can come back to the outer world experience. Notice the "things" around you, but also notice the space surrounding everything. Like the space between these words on the page. Or notes in music. We are forever surrounded by space.

Feeling Into the Human Experience

In the beginning was the Tao.
All things issue from it;
All things return to it.[9]

Whether you were already an energy, a "something" or not, who did you come through? Who was your mother? Your father? How did they adapt to your presence?

If your parents are not available to ask, think back to anything you may have heard, or even the atmosphere you may have felt when the subject of your birth or early years came up. What comes up in you now when you think about it?

Many of us don't remember our earliest days, months, or even years. My own memories don't really begin until around the age of seven. But there were picture albums I'd look at, of this baby (that was me??) being held by my young, smiling parents, wine bottles on the table or sitting out on their little Roman terrace, and it was like looking into an alternate universe.

Whomever that baby was, it didn't feel like me. Those parents weren't particularly the parents I knew, although I liked

---

[9] Lao-Tzu, trans. Stephen Mitchell, "Chapter 52," in Tao Te Ching: A New English Version (New York, NY: HarperPerennial, 1988).

seeing them smiling and looking so happy, living a life that seemed so much more about them than about me.

A good friend of mine was the third child born to Canadian prairie farmers. She has done a lot of training around the prenatal experience, supporting people in going back to a preverbal consciousness before their self-awareness became clear and separate.

In one of her own experiences exploring prenatal life, she went back to an awareness shortly after her conception — and became immersed in an energy of pure joy and excitement: the absolute wonder of her unadulterated potential, readying to come into being.

Then in the midst of this purity of joy came a different tone: a sudden shadow, a darker coloration penetrating her excitement. As her delight was split with this alternate awareness, she realized that this "other" energy wasn't hers; it came from a different source. It came from her mother, the moment she discovered she was once again pregnant.

Instead of mirroring pure excitement and joy, her mother, who already had two very small children and wasn't quite ready to begin a third, was flooded with disappointment. Of feeling "Oh no, not pregnant again!"

The tiny seedling, already coming into the human awareness, felt this disappointing energy like the pricking of a balloon. Rather than matching her buoyant energy, her mother met the discovery with regret; and my friend's eager anticipation was flattened by the sense of sinking sadness.

Is this how it goes for us all? Emerging from pure energy, we soon experience introductory lessons into the ever-changing nuances of emotion that this human journey will bring to us. Our earliest introduction to the vast human experience happens while still in the womb, bathing in the ever-flowing changes of our own mother's inner life.

My friend's mother did go on to accept this pregnancy and to love her new child dearly, eventually welcoming several more children into the world — so the disappointment wasn't a permanent state for either mother or baby. And yet...

When my friend, a cranial-sacral therapist well-versed in supporting the healing of traumas, discovered this in her own energy field of body-memory, she felt a visceral shocking sadness. Like her first fall from innocence, a shadowing of the pure energy from which she came.

Although we may enter this human experience with buoyant readiness, our lives are designed to span the gamut of emotions, the spectrum of experiences, the great panoply of opposites and all that lies in between.

Is there a loss in this? It can feel sad to think that we must lose touch so early with our original, expansive pure consciousness and become embroiled in the conflicts and confusion that are part of a human journey. What could be the point of this diversity? Perhaps we are looking at a paradigm whose infinite variety is actually for our benefit — even when aspects of it feel so very wrong.

Consider this: It is within the ever-changing world of contrasts, of separations and distinctions of feelings and experiences, that our potential for growth is inspired. Without friction, without challenges, the impetus for your evolution remains small.

Only through the infinite complexity of experience and feelings that we each will live, do the finely tuned masterpieces of ourselves gradually emerge.

Feeling Joy

Somewhere underneath, despite our movements, exposures and experiences, despite the people, situations, and crises, we still have access to joy, excitement, anticipation, and buoyancy. We may have lost awareness of them; we may have become so affected by the hurts and wrongs of human life that we are influenced away from them, and yet they remain.

It may seem superficial or even irresponsible to deliberately seek a feeling of joy in a world full of suffering. It may seem to invalidate our own suffering, or that of others, to consciously tune away from the wrongs and nurture a spark of joy within us. And yet, by remaining aligned with all the hurts and wrongs and traumas we have lived, we stay stuck perpetuating them within our own energy system. We breed further resentment and anger and hatred and fear — for ourselves, and for others.

How about experimenting a little? How about giving your system a chance to experience, even if just for a moment, what has never stopped being available within you. The feeling of joy.

Sit quietly and think for a moment, looking through your life for a time when you felt joy.

It was likely inspired by something — a beloved pet for example, or a perfect moment with someone you loved, or an experience in nature or listening to a particular piece of music.

You will find something — perhaps many things! Pick one and go to that moment in your mind.

Close your eyes and see that moment.
Where were you?
Who were you with?
What was around you?

Get very specific in seeing the details of that moment. Bring it into full color.

Notice other aspects of the moment.
Was there a particular fragrance in the air?
A feeling of something on your skin?
Were you eating something delicious or touching something wonderful?
What sounds were there in the background?

Immerse yourself more and more, using all of your senses, into that experience.
Continue to fill it out for yourself in as many dimensions as possible.

Notice what you are feeling in your body right now, as you move back into that moment.

How does it feel inside? Take your time and really focus on the physical sensations within you as you return to that experience.

And now — deliberately fill your heart with joy. Open yourself completely to the feeling, the emotion, of joy. Place all your attention there and remain fully focused on this feeling as you remain within the memory of that experience.

This may take some attention; we aren't used to deliberately creating a feeling — a positive feeling — for ourselves, so don't be surprised if this is challenging. But keep going, keep opening yourself to the feeling of joy.

Now let the other aspects of the moment fade, and just keep your attention on the feeling of joy.
Joy for its own sake.
Joy for the hell of it.
Joy because you can!
Stay with it, stretching it out... Stay with joy...
Stay with joy...
Notice how you feel about this. About deliberately cultivating joy.
Does your mind have a different opinion on this?
Does it feel you shouldn't be doing this?

You can watch your mind but stay disengaged from the thoughts. Focus on keeping your energy untouched by anything other than joy.

Stay loyal to joy.
Feel it radiating from your heart, your gut.
Feel it moving throughout your body.
Feel it expanding beyond you, into the world.
Feel joy permeating your original essence, your original energy.
Know joy. Be joy. Embody joy.

Remember what this feels like.

How easy was this for you to do? If it was difficult, then consider whether you have become used to looking for what's wrong in life, rather than appreciating what's right.

Notice if you feel resistance. It's a courageous act to reach for joy in the midst of a world that focuses so much attention on what's wrong. If we listen to the news at night, feeling joy can almost seem irresponsible.

For our own well-being and that of others, though, we should try to balance the sufferings of the world with regular forays into joy. Into peace. Into contentment. Because just as surely as we came into the world, we will one day leave it — and all the possibilities we could have lived, all the joy and enlivenment we could have felt, all the appreciation we could have offered to ourselves and others in our lifetime, will no longer be there.

When we focus our attention on something, we are potentiating it. We make it more available to our experience. Begin to explore choosing how you want to feel. Begin to return your own awareness to that original reality: the joy of simply being alive.

Rooting Our Humanness

We float in the womb, in the sea of our mother's moment-to-moment experiential reality. Our fetal nervous system absorbs her infinite feeling moments, long before we have language to describe our awareness. The world begins its subtle influence upon us, chemical signals express delivered courtesy of the placenta and amniotic fluid. Signals, regardless of what they transmit, we received from our earliest development.

The preliminary education of an earthly life dovetails with the development of our bodies as we gestate within the mother. No matter how welcomed and loved, every being growing into a human body will experience a nine-month-long apprenticeship in humanity, filtered through their expanding cellular network.

Neuroscientists have discovered that a certain amount of our mother's stress accelerates our physical and mental development. We seem meant to be exposed to stress for our own benefit. Perhaps this preliminary exposure to the human experience is as important a part of our gestation as the delivery of nutrients and the removal of waste. By the time we enter the world, we have been neurologically pre-wired, jump-started by mother and all she is living, as it streams through our sensory awareness.

It's something to consider that parts of ourselves were set in motion by the very circumstances, experiences, and situations our parents, especially our mothers, had during the nine months we grew within her. And in turn was she affected during her gestation by her mother. And her by the mother before. And before her. All the way back through our human origins it goes, one mother at a time.

We are compilations of the history of humankind itself, silently passed on within the infinite wombs that have gestated all humanity.

It's tempting to think that every child deserves a completely loving and welcoming womb time, that this is some kind of human right. And yet — there will never be a completely perfect nine-month scenario within which to grow a new human being. Perhaps that's why the idea of a test tube baby is both so tempting and so horrible.

To deliberately control every aspect of creation, of gestation, within the sterility of a laboratory watched over by white-coated technicians, is the worst kind of science-fiction imaginable.

It appears we humans are meant to be messed around with, to feel the entire spectrum of emotions, to explore and stumble and encounter hardship and stress right from the beginning. To learn about what does and doesn't feel good. To be indoctrinated into a worldview that reflects the history and experience of the family into which we are born.

What to do if you believe your mother was not in the best way during your pregnancy? What to do if you know or suspect that she went through difficult or traumatic events while you were gestating within? How to approach your own earliest beginnings with the intention of finding something good or beneficial for yourself, even though you might have preferred a very different pre-birth environment?

Remember that each of us has come to live, in one capacity or another, a hero's journey — where hardships are necessary parts of the adventure. Where confusion and even pain are signposts that we are in the vicinity of a challenge specific to us.

Notice what your thoughts are about your mother. About her mothering of you, whether as a child or even today. Regardless of how wonderful or terrible she might have been, many of us will have mixed feelings about her. We know too much, we swam in her waters — so to feel pure, unconditional love may be a challenge!

Often the best way to soothe confused feelings regarding our mothers is first to simply acknowledge and normalize them — even welcome them, as they have usually been relegated to the basement of our psyches, wallowing in a murky sea of anger, resentment, sadness, confusion, or guilt.

What would it feel like to touch those places of painful energies and simply embrace yourself as both the child as well as the adult you are today, despite the complexity of feelings you may have about your mother?

What would it be like to open yourself in a compassionate welcoming of what seemed to have gone wrong, and simply be willing to consider this was all part of your hero's journey?

Consider this: Do the influences and experiences you have suffered mean that something went irreparably wrong? That you were harmed or affected beyond healing or redemption? Or were these challenges you were born with the full capacity to take on?

Who Was Your Mother Before You?

Perhaps you have a picture of your mother. It can be an actual picture, or you simply see her in your mind's eye. Look at the picture for a minute, and then close your eyes, but keep her face clearly in your mind.

Look deeply at her, at the expression on her face. The depth within her eyes. Spend a minute simply gazing into her eyes. What are you feeling? Be present to what is happening within you.

Stay with what you experience, and if anything feels unpleasant, just open yourself up a little more; create as much inner space as you need. You are lifting the lid off the box labeled "Mother," so just stay with whatever you are feeling, as you gaze at her.

Take this gently. If you begin to feel very disquieting emotions, then this might be enough for today. Recognize there are some conflicted places within you around your mother and that in time, perhaps you will be more ready to explore further. Simply thank yourself for your courage to even approach this. There is nothing further you have to do right now. Take a few deeper breaths, and when you feel more settled, gently return to your outer life.

If, however, you feel comfortable gazing in your mother's eyes, you can go a little further. Remain very present to whatever you are feeling within yourself.

Imagine you could see beyond the visual surface of your mother and look into the story of her life. Into the feelings and situations, into those places and circumstances you know about her.

Perhaps specific memories will come up, or stories, or perceptions. Or maybe very little comes up, only things you have imagined. Keep looking at her face, into her eyes.

Now, begin to consider all that you don't know about your mother.

Imagine your mother as a baby herself. Tiny. Vulnerable. With her parents or caregivers.
What do you feel?
Do you notice anything?
Stay present to whatever you are experiencing within yourself, as you contemplate your mother's beginnings.

Now see your mother as a small child. Perhaps you know something of her early life, perhaps you know nothing. Simply be present to whatever comes forward into your awareness about your mother's earliest years on the planet.

And then move forward to her as a teenager.
What might she have been interested in?
What might she have been dreaming about for herself? What were her living conditions? What were the options she had available to her?

Now go forward still. Perhaps to her exploring relationships, exploring all the new steps further into the world she was taking as she entered adulthood.

Follow whatever you discover as you move forward through the imaginings of her life.
What did she dream for herself?
What did she believe was possible?
What opportunities did she have and what opportunities might have been denied?

Notice whatever you are feeling within yourself as you go through this imagined journey of your mother's life. Be very present to your feelings without judging, without questioning.

You may notice some discomfort coming up — just allow it, just be present to it without necessarily buying into it.

So often we know our parents in terms of what they weren't for us, rather than what they were. How they couldn't, rather than what they could. So just be present both to what you are exploring of your mother's early life BY (Before You) as well as the feelings evoked within you. Allow it all.

Now go to the moment when your energy coalesced into the call to come to earth. To the space of creation. To the beyond time connection that drew you together, the mutual desire, whether recognized or not.

Imagine you and your mother, not as the people you are or were, but as the impulses of growth, of forward motion, of potential and evolution, meeting in a profound communion.

Be present to whatever you are feeling, as here often there is no sense of language, only sensation. Perhaps emotion but notice if that is more a projection from your shared history, rather than the pure moment of creation between you.

No matter what has since taken place between you and your mother, your emergence and life destiny depended on this partnership, this connection, with her. Without her ultimate consent, you would not be here, you would not have this life. She opened to whatever changes your coming would bring to her. She became the portal through which you entered this world.

How does that feel?

Perhaps there are things you would like to say to her, or perhaps not.

Recognize that we are working in the energetic realm where our energy is already speaking, is already communicating; words aren't always necessary.

Just sit within this energy of you and your mother as co-partners in the on-going evolution of each of you.

Sit in her ultimate agreement, regardless of what else was going on in her life at the time. Or what happened immediately afterward, or has gone on to happen since.

Just remain present to the moment when you both agreed.

Michael Berold, a gifted facilitator in Family Constellation work, shared this phrase with me as a kind of resolution to painful parent/child dynamics. If you are noticing some disquieting feelings coming up, try these words:

"Thank you. You gave me my life, and that is a lot. I can take it from here."

Just sit and let these words resonate within you. No matter how terrible or wonderful your mother is or was; your relationship with her is or was; she was always doing the best she could with wherever she was in her life. Above all else, though, in the best way she could, she made room for you to be here.

Whatever you are feeling, allow and bring as much kindness and compassion to yourself, to your mother, to her life, and to your own, as you can. Rest in this place.

Perhaps later, you may feel like writing, dancing, or creating a piece of art or music to embody anything you may have discovered from this exploration. Allow yourself to take it in, to give it form, to express in whatever way honors your experience — and that of your mother's.

To Be — Or Not?

In a first pregnancy, everything feels unknown and foreign. When you can still fit into your clothes, it's hard to believe there is anything going on inside, other than feeling you have the stomach flu and are exhausted all the time. Perhaps because my pregnancy had been so unexpected and accompanied so quickly by getting married, I had trouble connecting the changes in my body with the development of an actual baby.

Apart from my dream time, with the portent of something beyond myself coming in, I mostly felt a strange combination of disconnection and deep connection — alternating back and forth between my outer and inner worlds.

I was still working of course, and still walking back and forth from the apartment to the office in Midtown Manhattan, a distance of a few miles. Then one day I noticed some blood on my underwear.

What did this mean? Was this something to worry about? What should I do? One more new unknown, one more question of what was normal, and what wasn't.

I had originally wanted a home birth with a midwife rather than going the specialist gynecological-oriented-hospital route. Home births were rare and deemed unsafe, so I relented on that — but found a midwife who delivered in the hospital and was a perfect combination of medical expertise and personal attention. She was also, blessedly, available for questions and concerns anytime of the day or night. Calling her, she immediately told me to get off my feet, and we made an appointment for the next day.

I followed her instructions — pregnancy inspires the protection mode, no matter how confused a woman may be within the experience — and the next day, Maureen and I both listened to the heartbeat going strong. Shortly thereafter, an ultrasound confirmed the baby's viability.

I took a week off work to lay around and the bleeding eventually stopped. But I had now been ushered into another aspect of expectant motherhood: the fear that something threatened this precious, yet still tentative, new life.

How many babies have been lost throughout time? How many births end prematurely or even full term with the worst kind of disappointment? How many mothers go from one day full of new life, to an empty vacuum the next? Later I would go on to have two miscarriages, so learned firsthand the heartbreak of a suddenly empty womb. But this was my first brush with danger.

Our fears are not unfounded. They have their history in our mothers, our grandmothers, the lineage linking one mother to the next, no matter what nationality or culture.

To lose a child. It implies we have done something wrong; we have squandered ourselves, ignored our duty, been irresponsible. And yet rarely does it have anything to do with us, but is an outcome of forces and energies beyond our awareness — and certainly beyond our control.

The history of uncertainty around childbearing — the possibility of miscarriage or stillbirth, of malformations or defects — has inspired huge developments in maternal care and medical assessments, interventions, and testing. As humans, we hate to have uncertainty; we lose sleep or feel uneasy when we can't know something to be okay, to be "normal." But no matter how far our medical abilities progress, no matter how much we can monitor every single aspect of pregnancy and delivery, there is something about this process that remains beyond our control.

No matter our technology, birth is always, intimately, connected to what we call death. The coming and the going remain two sides of the same coin. Miracle and mystery, something seems to come forward, but then recedes back into nothingness.

And death will have its way with us all, so it should be no surprise that even in procreation, losses will happen. For mothers who have already born a child, the assumption is that they will get over it, they already have a child so what's the big deal? Believe me, it's always a big deal.

For mothers who were awaiting their first child, the confusion, sadness, disappointment, and even embarrassment can never be underestimated. We cannot survive if our heart is ripped out of us; it is central to our lives.

A baby in the womb is like a second heart — it IS a second heart — whose beating has grown out of our own. We are breathing it, nourishing it, enveloping and protecting it — trusting in its life force as well as the safe harbour of our body for its growth.

When something goes amiss, when there is a misfiring in the unfolding of the design and the second heartbeat within us is extinguished, we move beyond the scope of logic or justification, or even explanation. There is a crack in the world, there is a loss that cannot be measured or made up. There is a grieving that will be done — that MUST be done.

Hopefully, we come to a time of laying down any guilt or railing at God. What was becoming manifest had gone as far into the process as it was going to go. In the move toward new life, something always remains beyond our human control.

How do you think your mother adapted to her pregnancy with you? Did she already have other children to be caring for? Would she have been given any special attention or was she full on with the rest of her life while incubating you? Were there any scary times for her? Had she lost children or pregnancies previously? What might she have been thinking about while carrying you?

And for you, the budding human, can you imagine what you might have been experiencing during your womb-time? What kind of energies were influencing your development, both of your own generating as well as those received from your mother? Were there crises, or major life changes? Deaths or separations? Large decisions being made, or were you gestated within the ongoing regularity of lives well-entrenched on a fixed course?

Creating a Foundation of Safety

Because bringing a new life into the world is never a sure thing; because your mother and father may have felt various measures of powerlessness in other areas of their lives; because the human experience offers a huge variety of threats and dangers, likely you were bathed in a certain amount of fear and trepidation about even coming into the world.

Don't take it personally! The world can feel even scarier when you are growing a baby at the same time you are juggling all the other balls of your life in the air.

Let's assume you received a fair share — maybe even more than a fair share — of stress or anxiety messages while in the womb. And that your nervous system obediently wired itself along those lines, with neural pathways primed to sense danger and respond accordingly — even when the environment is actually benign and even welcoming. What to do about that?

Let's again approach our inner workings from within, but instead of directly putting in mental messages, we're going to go to a different part of the body — the part of us that is most connected to the earth, to grounding, to stability, to security — and which is often where our first perceptions of danger are perceived, whether justified or not.

Sit comfortably — this exercise is better done sitting in a chair with your feet on the floor, rather than lying down — and once again, close your eyes. Turn your attention inward, away from the outer world with all its many distractions and activities, and instead notice your breath.

Discover that you are breathing! That in itself can be quite surprising! Amidst everything that is going on in your life, amidst all your busyness and doing, you have been continuing to breathe! And you didn't even have to think about it! It just happens, all by itself!

Tune into this whole breathing thing.
Notice how you are breathing.
How deep into your body does your breath go?
How long are the inhales? The exhales?
Take a few moments and just discover more intimately what your breathing is like.

(If you have been breathing through your mouth, do your best to switch over to nose breathing. For some people this is hard, so if you feel you can't get enough air, then "sip" the breath in through just a corner of your mouth slowly and steadily. Try to exhale it through your nose. Over time, try to completely inhale through your nose, at least on every other breath. But only push yourself as far as is comfortable.)

Now gradually invite the inhales a little deeper into your body. Don't force anything, just gently envision the breath going deeper, your lower ribcage expanding. And then a bit more deeply, expanding on the inhale, contracting as you exhale. Keep this gradual deepening of the breath going by gently, gently inhaling deeper into your body, into your lower abdomen.

As the breath moves in deeper, pay attention to your exhales. Gradually lengthen the exhales, extending them a bit further, releasing all of your breath.

If this is feeling difficult, if you are feeling any sense of anxiety or stress, here is a little variation called the straw breath. Continue to pursue these deeper inhales, but on the exhale, "blow" the breath out through your pursed lips — as though you were blowing through a straw. Blow out all the air this way, and then begin your next inhale. Keep this up for a minute or more until you notice you are feeling much more relaxed.

Notice what you are feeling inside. You may eventually reach an inner state of calm.

Continuing to breathe in deeply, following with long, slow exhales, turn your attention to the bottom of your feet. Feel where they connect to the ground or floor beneath you.

Notice where the bottom of each toe meets the floor; where the soles of your feet meet the floor; the heels.
Feel the sturdiness of the ground supporting your feet.

What does this feel like? Do you sense anything in your feet? Where they meet the ground? Imagine your feet spreading out on the ground, fully supported, fully rooted.

Our feet get so little attention. What does it feel like to focus completely on them, to bathe them in your attention? To appreciate how they connect you to the earth, how they allow you to walk upright and to move through the world?

Keeping your attention still peripherally on the bottoms of your feet and the ground, now begin to include the rest of your feet in your awareness.
The sides and tops of your feet.
Your ankles.
Try not to lose awareness of where your feet are planted on the ground, as you expand your consciousness up; remain connected to the earth, even as you include more of your body in your perception.

Now move to include your lower legs.
Your calves.
Your knees.
Keep checking back with the bottoms of your feet on the floor,
as you expand upward.
To your thighs.
Your hips.
Your pelvic floor.
And now just stay here, remaining very present to this whole
lower part of your body — from your feet connected to the
ground, up through your legs to your pelvic floor, hips, sacrum
of your spine.

As you continue to be very aware of this part of your body, sit
in these words: I am safe. It is safe to be here.
Notice if anything comes up. If so, don't resist, but instead be
open to whatever feelings are coming up and embrace them
within your awareness. Soothe them, allowing the words "I am
safe. It is safe to be here" to continue resonating within you.

Keep your attention on this lower part of your body, continuing
to sit in the resonance of the words, in the deep regularity of
your breath.
Safe.
Secure.
It is right that I am here.
I am welcome here.
I am safe here.

If parts of you seem to come up in contradiction, don't be
surprised. Not having a basic sense of safety is something many
of us came in with. It probably goes back to your mother or
father, or their mother or father, or to the ones before them.

But now, sitting here in a safe, calm place, with your feet firmly planted on the floor, supported by the earth beneath you and the chair on which you sit, you can begin to cultivate a fuller sense of safety for yourself.

Let the words resonate in this lower part of your body. Feel them in the base of your spine.

What does that feel like? You may feel a sense of warmth or expansion. Or especially if your sense of safety is quite precarious, you may feel some unease. Or you may feel nothing at all.

Whatever your experience, try not to judge, try to not force something that doesn't yet feel true.

Just acknowledge you, like everyone else, is a work in progress.

Just because you are here, just because you managed to make it onto the planet and live the number of years you have lived, doesn't mean your nervous system isn't still kind of worried about this whole life thing ... cut yourself some slack. You are doing just fine. [10]

---

[10] However, if your body resists feeling any sense of safety and your nervous system is very clear that threat is part of your life, investigate whether there is something unsafe in your current reality. Don't try to convince yourself that you are safe, when it isn't actually true. Use this exercise and your awareness to make whatever changes you need to make to safely remove yourself as a target within a dangerous environment. You are here to live your life — not to sacrifice your unique purpose to someone else's misguided pain and control.

Birthing Influences

Like many women pregnant with their first child, everything was new and I sought as much information as possible. No internet in those days, but an unending supply of books provided insight into what was happening within me — and what to expect next.

My first trimester was so busy, and I felt so rotten, that just getting through one day to the next was enough. But in the second trimester, with the wedding behind me, I began to consciously settle into the truth of this baby taking shape within.

Going into a department store, I found myself wandering around the baby department. Caressing the softness of infant blankets or stuffed animals. Looking at the little outfits. Sleepers, socks. I had never seen anything so tiny.

My parents lived far from New York City, so they didn't play a big hands-on part in those months, although we had lots of phone calls and much excitement. My mother's own precarious birthing history never entered into our conversation, nor did she seem anxious about the delivery of my upcoming baby. In fact, when I first told her I was pregnant, she caught her breath and then said, "Oh Susie, it will be the most wonderful experience of your LIFE!"

At a monthly checkup with my midwife, I met a mother in the waiting room with her three-year- old daughter and infant baby boy. Connecting easily, I asked her how the delivery had gone. "Well!" she said. "We actually made it to the hospital this time." What? I leaned forward; here was something important.

At the end of her first pregnancy, she woke up in the middle of the night in advanced labor. No time to get to the hospital, her husband phoned midwife Maureen and she coached them through delivering their daughter right there in the bed. Wow! The most natural thing in the world!

With their second baby, they were better prepared. When they recognized the early signs of labor, there was no waiting around at home. Off to the hospital, where he was born as planned, without incident.

This story thrilled me! Everything I'd read, everything I'd heard, was about how long the first baby takes. How protracted the labors are. How you should stay home as long as possible because it will take hours and hours before the baby is actually ready to be born.

But here — a totally different experience! Imagine — sleeping through those early stages of labor, and then — boom! Welcome baby!

I asked Maureen about her patient's experience. She laughed, saying yes, it had been quite a surprise! And inside me, I knew — this was the kind of birth I wanted.

There was a reason that mother had been in the waiting room when I was there — to tell me her story and let it take root in my own field of possibilities, overriding all the other birthing stories coming my way. There were many ways for a baby to be born, and deep within me, a new connection was being made.

That meeting felt pivotal, laying down a new pathway through the neural, chemical, emotional, and energetic channels of communion humming between my baby and myself. I could do this birth, and it would be empowering and satisfying.

A woman's body is built around an energetic template designed to bring forth a child. Not all women will or can give birth, and every woman has her own unique version of that template. Some will need significant intervention and assistance in a multitude of aspects around conception, gestation, and delivery of a live child — but the energetic blueprint remains.

You were born from a woman's body, as was I. We have all been pushed or pulled or lifted out from a place that has grown too narrow into a place that likely felt all too big. Whether someone is dropped in a field or removed under operating lights in a surgical theater, we all transit from a hushed inner sanctum into a bright, noisy, and chaotic world. The journey of us all, enacted how many quadrillion, quintillion, sextillions of times, through how many gazillions of women's bodies. And each time, a miracle.

Your mother's body was so much more than simply the vessel. She was the yielder, the one who had to give over and let YOUR development take its course. So much for her to think about in the months during your development. So much for her to anticipate, so much that would be unknown. That would have to be handled in the moment, trusting in the body, the baby, the design — and if a break in that design happened, trusting that the appropriate help would be there.

Mothers each have their own individual story, as they brought the uniqueness of you into the world in whatever way you emerged. Every birth is a complete story, with a beginning, a middle, and an end. No part of the story can be foretold. It will be what it will be.

PART III
The Birthing Process

Emerging Into the World

My due date was still over a month away. It was January in New York, with slushy roads and cold temperatures. My boss was away, and I had an appointment uptown with the obstetrician who was Maureen's backup, should things get complicated during labor. I left the office early and ambled toward the Upper East Side, going in and out of shops and acquiring multiple bags along the way. Eventually I arrived at the doctor's office and was shown in.

The obstetrician examined me — and was surprised! I was already four centimeters dilated, the baby's head was down and fully engaged. He informed me that this examination alone might serve to bring on labor. Likely the baby would be born in the next few days!

My reaction? Elation! I was tired of being pregnant, awkward, and bulky, and could hardly wait to meet this baby. I was impatient and fully focused on their arrival. His words reignited that sense of confidence I felt at the prospect of giving birth. It was about to happen!

Mindful I should conserve my energy for what was now imminent, I took the bus home. These days on public transit, people would immediately stand and offer me a seat — a bonus of late pregnancy.

Sitting and looking out the window as we drove through Central Park, I noticed my abdomen regularly hardening for a few seconds, and then relaxing. Known as Braxton-Hicks contractions, they had been happening sporadically over the last few weeks, and are normal in the later stages of pregnancy. But these were more regular. Was labor beginning?

Once home, I called Dennis. It was a Thursday afternoon and he had been planning to fit in one more weekend of skiing in Vermont before the birth. Excitedly I blurted out: "You can't go skiing this weekend! We're going to have the baby! And the doctor thinks it's happening now!"

Silence. And then, "Wow! Do I still have time for my squash game before I come home tonight?" Yes, fine!

Much later I learned that after hanging up, he told his colleague sitting at the next desk that it looked like the baby was about to come. Mike, not yet a parent, but having watched multiple friends go through the dramas of first babies, wisely shook his head. "Don't get too excited," he said. "I bet a month from now you are still waiting."

With those calming words, Dennis went off to play squash.

Meanwhile, I called Maureen. The painless contractions were regular, and she was quite surprised to hear what the doctor had said. "Just lie down and rest," she told me, "Let's try and put this off a few more days."

"NO WAY!!" I responded. "This baby is ready, and so am I!" She laughed and said, "Okay, keep me posted. When the contractions are five minutes apart, call me."

Being four weeks early, we hadn't even attended all our child birthing classes, including the all-important ones on labor and delivery. When Dennis got home, I sat him down, gave him dinner (I was too excited to eat) and opened to the chapter on birthing in the famous *What to Expect When You're Expecting* book.

He needed to get up to speed quickly, as my contractions were regular and getting closer together. We watched TV for a bit, although I kept jumping up and down, too pumped to focus on anything other than timing the still completely painless contractions. Around 9 p.m., when they were indeed five minutes apart, Maureen told us to get to the hospital.

We gathered all the things we had been instructed to bring — so much stuff, we had to put it all in garbage bags! The multiple pillows, bags for ice, my own bag, the bag for the baby, diapers, etc. etc. and went out to hail a taxi.

The driver knew nothing about our purpose. Delighted with the absence of traffic, he barrelled down Ninth Avenue, hitting every pothole and gunning every light. When he pulled up to the front door of St. Vincent's Hospital and we were struggling out with all our stuff, I told him jubilantly "I'm going to have a baby tonight!"

His face literally went white. "Dios Mio!" he exclaimed. "If I had known that, I would have driven so much slower!" He shook Dennis's hand, wished us luck, and probably stayed under the speed limit for the rest of the night.

We went up to the maternity area where Maureen was waiting and into the birthing room. St. Vincent's was an old hospital, drafty, with an old-fashioned radiator clanging out the heat. We organized our stuff and Dennis went off to get everyone sandwiches for the long night ahead.

Maureen checked me out. The contractions remained regular and close together — and still painless! I was high with excitement! My baby's arrival was imminent, my body was doing the work, and there was no discomfort at all, just like I had imagined!

Maureen remained impassive. Although labor had progressed, she was mindful that this was an early baby who shouldn't go through the undue stress of a prolonged labor, so she broke my waters. And then, almost instantly, everything narrowed — and down the rabbit hole I went.

The intensity of childbirth will be experienced differently by every woman but no matter how much it may be altered by drugs or other interventions, it is an overwhelming journey. The start of a contraction is a subtle gathering of focused sensation, which then expands, grows, spreading out until it rises to the overwhelming shrieking peak of endurance...and then gradually, blessedly, subsiding down into relief.

You lose track of time; everything revolves around the arising, the surviving, the recovery from the incessant, never-ending rounds of pain that keep coming over and over again.

You are certain that your body is being torn, split in two, as you are told, encouraged, yelled at, to push. To push harder. To push longer. To keep on pushing, the urgent voices around you fading into the background as you are working harder than you have ever worked before in your life, while you are hurting more than you have ever hurt.

Giving birth takes you over and churns you up into pieces, fragments. A process that once started, cannot be stopped.

When it seems that there is nothing left to give, you give once more. You push once more. The words vaguely heard — there's the head! You push. The words — a little more, push a little more — and you push. And sweat. And maybe poop. And grit your teeth, making noises like you have never made before.

And then, once the head and the shoulders have emerged, suddenly, very quickly, there is your baby.

After thirty-six weeks of shared space, a baby emerged from my body at 12:28 a.m., barely three hours after stepping out of that taxi.

I was lying back exhausted, trying to catch my breath, relieved beyond anything that it was over, while Dennis, Maureen, and the nurses examined the baby.

"It's a boy, right?" I asked, eyes still closed.

"No Sue, it's a girl," Dennis said.

What?

"Oh, come on, I know it's a boy. Stop kidding around!"

"No, Sue, it's a girl. It's really a girl."

A girl?

If I hadn't been so spent, I would have cried. Tears of joy and amazement. But also of confirmation. A boy was what I expected, what I would have been happy about and glad for Dennis. But a girl — somehow I had known this all along. Yet afraid to acknowledge lest I be wrong, lest I get disappointed. That energy I had felt some eight months earlier, and had been feeling and communing with in all the months since, that I had grown more and more excited to meet, had now emerged as I had somewhere always known she would. As our baby girl.

In my lifetime I have given birth to three baby girls — Hanna, Olivia, and Alexandra — and while each birth was overwhelmingly intense, they were about as perfect as a birth can be: fast, efficient, successful outcomes with no need of any medical intervention.

Although I haven't always handled other physical pain so graciously, I have been a champion in giving birth.

No matter how much medical science can mitigate or remove the physical pain, ease the discomfort, and minimize the trauma, there is a power to birth that goes beyond our full control.

Do you know anything about how you entered into the world? What kind of birthing situation your mother was in? How it went? You may have been told stories — and if there was trauma or danger involved in your emerging, this may still be held energetically in your body's memories.

If you know nothing about your birth (or perhaps never thought to ask), take a moment now and simply consider this great transition that you and your mother went through together.

No matter how your current relationship with her may be, or whether she is even still alive, know that in your birth, every ounce of her energy was dedicated to bringing you forward. No matter if she was drugged or numbed or cut open to help you out, no matter if she was a committed mother or exploring the more dysfunctional sides of life, her number one desire and her complete physical, emotional, mental, and even spiritual dedication in that experience was to see you safely into the world.

Filling in Gaps From Our Beginnings

At the beginning of this book, I related the story of my own birth. A seemingly normal delivery back in the days when husbands sat in the waiting room and babies went off to the hospital nursery. But then a sudden life-threatening situation with my mother hemorrhaging severely, my father having to source out the blood to save her life, and her weeks of recovery — while I remained away from her. Certainly not the beginnings that meet all the current standards of health and well-being for mother and baby!

Where was the immediate bonding, the latching onto the breast, the first ingestion of colostrum? Or the warm, drowsy days of lying around together with oxytocin flowing, as mother and baby fall completely in love with each other?

No, my beginnings were of separation, of the near-death of my mother, of a hands-off father, of the no doubt efficient but possibly impersonal care by the hospital nursery staff.

Fast-forwarding a few weeks, my mother had recovered enough to come home. Only then did we begin to get to know each other, and to settle in as a family of three. Whether or not there was any fallout from my earliest days, I retained no conscious or even shadowy memories of it.

However...

I was in the Netherlands at the intensive international Present Child immersion training. One day we did an exercise in returning to the time shortly after our birth. With representatives acting as our parents, we explored what our felt, pre-verbal psyche remembered from our first days as a separate human being.

In this work, just as in the meditations we have been sharing, there is no sense of "why" something is. This work is always done by deliberately turning away from the outer world, beta-focused consciousness, and instead accesses the beyond-time-and-space qualities of other, broader states. It is in these realms where more intuitive wisdom, a greater accessing, takes place for us. Nothing is questioned, all is allowed to unfold as it does, trusting in the deeper currents of insight. Whatever is ready to be revealed, will do so.

The lights in the room were dim, the voices muted. Without knowing why, it felt appropriate for me to place my parent representatives standing away, with their backs to me, while I lay down on the mat behind them.

Suddenly, without warning, my breathing became extremely difficult. I couldn't control my diaphragm. It, and my breath, began jerking all over the place. Extreme panic set in. It was as if my body didn't even know how to draw in a coherent breath. I was petrified, gasping in helplessness, my breath jerking and spastic, feeling I might die.

Meanwhile, my parents were right there but couldn't see or hear me — and I was so disconnected from the basic ability to breathe, that I couldn't make a sound.

"Call your parents to help," the assistant whispered, but it was impossible! I was trapped in this total stalemate of terrified dyskinesia while my parents were looking away, beyond my reach.

Finally the assistant herself had to instruct my "parents" to turn around, whereupon they both gathered me up in their arms and I dissolved into an ocean of tears and violent sobs. For what seemed like a long, long time, they held and soothed me. Slowly, finally drained of my terrified tears, my nervous system settled, and my breathing regulated. I was eased into calm.

What a surprise! The terror and helplessness that took me over were sudden, overwhelming, and uncontrollable. Could it be that my entrance into the world missed that step of coming to feel safe and regulated within my body? And now, years later, a part of my neurology still held the memory of such basic insecurity that even breathing was a question?

Looking back through my years, I could see how this perception had likely played out in a number of ways. Unconsciously looking for people who would take control because I didn't feel capable in myself. Retreating to the protection offered by stronger individuals — while at the same time, resenting the control I ceded over to them. Not trusting in my own sufficiency in the outer world.

In retrospect, I recognized all of this. But I also began to see that, bit by bit, my life had an undercurrent, a quiet dedication to discovering my own security, my own safety, my own ability to stand and move. A dedication toward restoring my own strength and power until what might have begun as a gap, became an impetus urging me forward on my personal hero's journey.

The experience of birth is the first major trauma in a young life, and within its passage from inner to outer, lie many variations. While many infants may transit this without issue and find their safety completely met, for others, it's not been such an easy entrance.

How do we know when we have remaining energies automatically screaming "DANGER!" due to nervous systems that free fall too easily into threat?

Regardless of where the origins come from, we can get clues by what triggers us to feel insecure in our lives. How do we respond in new situations? To other people? How easily can we believe in our dreams being realizable? How much are we willing to give to ourselves? How worthy do we feel in simply being alive?

If you notice — perhaps with a sinking sensation — that you do easily feel fear or lose your sense of security in life, don't despair. Our defense system's job is to keep us safe above all else, and clearly yours has done its job very well! But perhaps it's been wired into a higher pitch and needs a little soothing, a little conscious support in seeing life more through the lens of possibilities, rather than its dangers.

We are always works in progress; it's never too late to make changes in our wiring.

A Loving Welcome to the World

On our own, it can be extremely difficult, and perhaps not even safe, to try and dig into any birth traumas. Without some guidance from a supportive partner (whether personal or professional), it can be easy to retraumatize ourselves and become overwhelmed with those feelings of helplessness, hopelessness, terror, or whatever immersive experience an infant goes through as they make their way out from oneness to separation.

Rather than trying to journey back and excavate any of your own early traumatic moments, let's envision a loving welcome. Let's become the perfect parent, tenderly receiving your own infant newborn.

A little reminder:

Remember what these exercises are about: rewiring patterns laid down within us — within the very synapses of our brain and nervous system communication — that got created and emphasized around some kind of a perceived wrong, harm, lack, or loss. No matter how deep-seated this pattern of perception may still be within us, we can consciously, deliberately, discover a different interpretation — a kinder, more loving understanding — and begin to know that reality as our truth.

Notice what you feel even while reading the words of this exercise. If you feel any unease or downright repulsion, just take note of that — and proceed gently.

On the other hand, if you feel this exercise is boring, repetitive, or just plain stupid, give it a little space and see if something

*new, something that shines a more compassionate light
onto your earliest moments, can now come forward.*

*As we have done so many times, close your eyes and settle
yourself comfortably in a chair. Imagine you are present at the
most important introduction of all time, the most potent meeting you have ever had. You are about to meet and receive into
your arms, your own precious, infinitely beloved baby — who
is you, as you entered the world so long ago.*

*What are you feeling inside, as you wait for this moment? As
you prepare yourself for this meeting?*

*Notice any physical sensations you may be feeling. Pay attention
to them without judging; simply being aware and open.*

*What is happening in your stomach? Your chest? Wherever you
notice any physical sensations, open yourself to them in greater
awareness — and if your mind starts to tell stories about
anything, you can ask it to simply sit this one out for a while.
You are moving away from the here and now and entering a
timeless space.*

*Prepare for this meeting by focusing on your breath. Let it
become deeper. More regular. Take some time to allow your
breath to stabilize and ground you.*

What kinds of emotions are alive in you right now?

*Again, don't suppress anything or react in any way to what you
are feeling. Simply notice — if you are feeling some negative
or painful emotions, be extremely gentle with them, and with
yourself.*

*Recognize that you are exploring some deep and possibly still-
raw energies that are needing your loving acceptance.*

*We have all taken on lots of beliefs about ourselves —
our unworthiness, our wrongness, our badness, our
inappropriateness — and these may be coming up inside you.
Be gentle.*

*A baby is pure innocence, pure beingness. No matter what
has happened in your life since this moment, this is how you
entered the world. Innocent and pure.*

*Innocent and pure. Let these words resonate inside you, as you
approach yourself as newly born.*

*Perhaps in your inner eye you can actually see a baby. Notice
what he or she looks like.*
Their little fingers and toes, tiny ears, open eyes.
Their small, tender body.
*This is your body. The living vehicle through which you will
be experiencing all that lies ahead.*
This is you.

Be attentive to what the baby is feeling. Tune into their state.
*They have just come through a momentous challenge — they
may need you to help them recover and feel safe.*

Move toward this baby and gently lift them up into your arms.

*How is their body temperature? They are used to being
surrounded by the perfect temperature of amniotic waters —
so perhaps you can wrap them in a warm, soft blanket. Tuck it
around their tiny shoulders, under their little chin, around their
innocent body.*

How does it feel to hold this baby?
What is the sensation of actually holding them in your arms?
Would you like to gently rock this baby? Hum to them?

Notice what is happening in your body as you hold this baby.

What is happening in your heart?

*Allow yourself to fully open your heart to this tiny little being, this **you**, in all your infant innocence and purity.*

Yes there is helplessness, but also — can you feel your strength? Your potential? All the possibilities ahead for this little baby? All the learning and unfolding that will take place on his or her journey?

Remain present to your own emotions as you hold this baby.

What do they need?

Usually a baby simply needs to be held close, to feel your warmth, your loving attention, your wholehearted willingness to be there with them.

So do that. No matter what your own early moments or days may have been like, this is an opportunity to fill in any gaps that might have happened during your entrance; to complete anything that couldn't have been completed back then.

Fill in any gaps. Hold this precious baby. Love them tenderly. Completely. Cherished, safe, protected, let yourself be your perfect parent.

Stay with yourself and this baby for as long as is comfortable. When you feel some sense of completion — or want to move on with your day — perhaps you would like to tuck this baby into your heart, to take them with you as you go out into the world. Or not. Respect whatever feelings you have.

We may not remember our birth consciously, but our body does. Trust and accept whatever you have experienced. Be gentle with yourself.

How was this exercise for you? Did you feel connected to the infant you, or did you feel some conflicting emotions? Did you go numb or check out of the exercise? Did you feel threatened?

Take your time to process whatever you experienced. In time, you may want to write or draw a representation of this. Maybe you even feel like moving your body — there may be some powerful energy alive in you, that movement will help release.

Especially if you felt some discomfort, allowing the feelings to be expressed through your body or other creative avenues can help release long-held energy, and open up room for something new.

This doesn't happen instantly, but with gentle attention and self-compassion, you are making new connections to this pure and innocent part of yourself.

Pay attention to how you felt and feel now — without any judgment. If you felt uncomfortable or numb or couldn't even go there, it's possible you have some stuck energy around your birthing experience that has never been integrated.

That's okay. You can return to this exercise anytime you feel ready to approach it again. You will know when the time is ripe. Let it happen all in good time.

PART IV

An Infant State
of Mind

Can you coax your mind from its wanderings
And keep to the original Oneness?[11]

I was driving home one afternoon. The highway is elevated and curves along the side of a mountain overlooking the ocean. It's a beautiful sight, but mostly I would be oblivious, wrapped up in whatever issues were occupying my beta mind.

But that afternoon the sun was setting, and the sky was covered in a stunning pastel sequence of oranges, pinks, and purples. The granite mountains etched their silhouette against it; the shimmering ocean stretched out below.

Suddenly I was overcome by such a deep sense of well-being. Everything else simply disappeared. My mind knew nothing other than the fullness of this moment: driving my car, immersed in this beauty. Expansive, wondrous, absolute. No thoughts separated me from my experience, everything was complete in that moment. Reality in all its fullness.

Then I reached my highway exit and within an instant, dropped back into my more practiced head space. Anticipating

---

[11] Lao-Tzu, trans. Stephen Mitchell, "Chapter 10," in Tao Te Ching: A New English Version (New York, NY: HarperPerennial, 1988).

what was waiting for me at home, dwelling on the people, issues, and needs all ahead, very quickly feeling the familiar tensions and conflicts replace that exquisitely satisfying sense of wholeness.

The Newborn Brain

The beta brain frequency is where we adults spend most of our waking hours. It's the practical, in-the-world frequency where we figure out the best ways to get things done: to do our jobs, put dinner on the table, juggle the multitude of demands that life is asking of us. It works lightening-fast to process what we think we know, in order to project how things will unfold going forward.

Without this highly useful frequency, the nuts and bolts of our lives would never come together to do our jobs, build that house, organize a government. But while the beta frequency is necessary to bring a sense of order in the world, it isn't particularly creative.

Beta brain relies on past experience to assess what will happen in the future. It doesn't have the bandwidth to imagine or expect new potential or possibilities. It remains perpetually drawing from the same information: what it already knows (or thinks it knows). We repeat a lot of history while in the beta state of mind, because every decision, response, or reaction stems from conclusions our brains have already made about life.

Day-to-day beta energy is busy doing, busy seeing an outer world of separate things that need to be controlled and problems that need to be solved. Beta mind fixates on what appears solid, what already is. When we are in beta brain, we are resonating with what we believe is the current situation, and our reaction to it.

What state of mind does an infant have? Clearly not the beta! Very tiny babies' brains are mostly in the delta frequency, where there is little awareness of an outside world, or of anything separate at all. They live in a perpetual present moment of sensory experience, free of language, assessments, or critical thinking.

A baby is coming from that state of fusion within the womb, still unaware of the earth in all its diversity, and the requirements of being a human in a body. These early days, weeks, and months are the transition time, when they remain highly connected to that fusional oneness, even as adjustments begin to be made. Their little bodies, brains, nervous systems, immune systems, and hormonal systems are all starting up. Bit by bit the focus changes, from the source waters of unity, to this external world of dense diversity.

Yet while these newly born little beings are living in the more unified consciousness of the delta vibrations, parents are mostly operating in the beta: Focused outwardly on solving problems, paying the rent, attending to their jobs, other children, or any number of things they are responsible for. Although the baby's whole world is their moment-to-moment experience, parents are definitely not in that same state.

Mothers are designed — hormonally, chemically, neurologically — to fall in love with and want to devote body and soul to supporting this helpless little being in their earth entry. But life doesn't always work out that way.

The birth may have been difficult and her own body recovering from injury or trauma. She may have other children, or need to go back to work, or simply be incapable due to her own life circumstances to fulfil the twenty-four/seven needs of this little being.

Wherever we come from, we're new to planet earth. After the months of gestation in a human womb, our exquisitely sensitive physical bodies emerge tiny, immature, dependent, and clueless to the world. Born to humans who are right in the middle of still figuring things out for themselves, and who can make only so much room for us.

No matter how dedicated and loving parents are, they are living in a different head space and reality than their baby, with a wide range of demands the external world continually imposes upon them.

We must accept that this is our design — whether you are a parent of children yourself, or from your perspective as an adult thinking back to your own infancy. This is how we humans make our way into the world.

Perhaps you have some vague sensory impressions that you imagine relate to your early days. If they feel uncomfortable, you aren't alone. While some of us may remember warmth and cozies from our introductory time on the planet, the moments that tend to stand out were the ones that weren't so comfortable. The ones that our nervous system took in and couldn't completely process, without some remaining red flags stuck in place.

Needs Not Always Met

If you are a parent, do you remember those early days with your infant? How they could sleep through anything? Or cry with such full-bodied distress? Likely you learned to recognize those cries, and their needs. You learned when they were expressing hunger or tiredness or a wet diaper. You noticed their emotions or reactions — perhaps startling at a loud noise or crying at the touch of something unpleasant. And then — the disappearance once more into a totally deep sleep.

Besides sleep, the greatest need in supporting these little beings' transition to life outside the womb is through what a mother's body is built to offer: human milk. Or for those who cannot provide it, a nourishing equivalent. Given while being held close, smelling the comforting, familiar smell of their mother or caregiver while the warm, sweet liquid is sucked into their tiny mouths and fills those delicate tummies.

For babies just born, being put to the mother's breast immediately after birth creates a safe transition, a soothing relief after the unrelenting pressure of being squeezed out into the world. The baby's suckling also stimulates the mother's release of oxytocin, the love hormone, into her milk. As it flows through them both, it naturally slows down the world, reuniting them into that sweet sense of oneness. Ideally these are days and weeks of feeding, napping, floating safely together.

Sheltered, just a bit longer, from the external demands of worldly life.

Once I had my first child and experienced the sweetness of our many months of breastfeeding — how we would gaze for long, blissful minutes into each other's eyes as she nursed, how I fell in love so completely and watched her growth unfolding literally within my arms — I began to recognize and mourn the loss of that for myself.

The stark imaginings of my beginnings — in the hospital nursery, bottle fed by nurses, far from my mother — took on a painful reality in my mind. As I moved forward in my own healing work with other parents, some of whom had painful or traumatic birthing experiences with their children, it was common to find feelings of loss or guilt clouding not only their memories of the birth experience, but also in how they related to their child going forward.

When this happens, it can be easy to remain stuck in those feelings that something wrong happened, that we were cheated or lost out on what should have been a different (i.e. better) experience. Looking to blame something or someone for not achieving the perfect birth we wanted to have. And yet...

The birth experience is only the beginning of our lives, our relationships, our stories. Finding something to appreciate in any part of our stories and deliberately rescripting aspects we feel went wrong, can help us stop recycling those hurts and instead discover so much to feel grateful for.

The only thing that keeps us stuck in regret or loss is ourselves. There are ways to change our inner stories, our inner beliefs. When we decide to finally free ourselves of our regrets, a funny thing happens. We free those others who were part of the "bad" story as well — our parents, our children, the medical professionals, even God — and allow a more accepting, compassionate reality to come forward.

My own experience in the Netherlands connected me to what might have been an unconscious, but still felt, consequence of my initial experience out in the world. Here is a process you can use for yourself, even if you have no idea about your own birth, to further soothe any turbulence you might have experienced.

*If you had a difficult birthing situation with your biological child, you could do this exercise two ways: first for your own birth, and then later, for your child's. Birth trauma runs through the history of humanity, so don't assume it was only your child's birth that holds some painful energy for you. Working directly to love yourself through any lingering pain from your personal birthing past will open you up to love away any regrets you may feel about your child's birth.

Meeting Our Needs with Love

We all came into the world through a human body designed to gestate, birth, and then care for us until we were developed enough to do for ourselves.

No matter how your actual experience of leaving the womb and adjusting to the outer world went, let's imagine the "best of all possible worlds" experience of being cared for within your perfect environment, providing all your needs with ease and love.

Sit quietly with plenty of time and privacy for yourself. This is a further grounding of the previous loving welcome into human life, wherein you and your helpless, vulnerable infant can relax together with all the time needed to adapt to this new adventure.

Sit quietly, comfortably. Close your eyes. Settle into yourself. Take some time to let go of the normal babble of thoughts in your mind. Focus on your breath. Tell your mind you are going to deliberately step away for just a little while, but not to worry; you will be back.

Breathing slowly and easily, allow yourself to turn away from the busyness of the outside world. Begin to open up some space in your imagination.

Consider, and begin to create, an earthly sanctuary.

It may be a place in nature.
It may be a place you have never seen, but can imagine. A place of quiet. Safety. Sanctity.
Where stillness and calm permeate the atmosphere.

Take some time and create, in your mind's eye, this beautiful, pristine environment.

Move into the experience of this serene and restful space.

What does it feel like to imagine yourself there? Look around more closely, and begin to attune to all that is in this space. The sights within it. Sounds. Perhaps smells. The textures of things within it. Become fully immersed here.

As you feel yourself in this space, imagine you are also there with the tiny infant you.

Imagine you are holding this baby.

Find a place for you both to be totally comfortable. Is there a perfect place to sit or lie down? Discover and settle into the most relaxing, supportive position you both can enjoy.

Experience yourself in this place, and feel the baby's response to it as well. Are they relaxed? Do they feel safe and secure? Make any adjustments to the space that either of you need, so there is nothing lacking.

Continue to immerse yourself more and more fully, paying attention both to your own comfort as well as the baby's.

Pay attention to what you are feeling in your body. Notice any sensations.
How are you breathing?
How does your stomach feel?
Your shoulders?
Perhaps scan your body. If there is any discomfort anywhere, ask yourself what you or the baby might need, to create an even safer, more restful space. Maybe the noises in the space need to be softened. Maybe you want to lock the door against

anyone else coming in. Adjust whatever you feel will maintain the complete safety and comfort of this space.

And now imagine that there is a Presence in this beautiful place that is there in complete devotion and attention to you — both the adult and the baby. You don't need to give this Presence a name, just feel their total attention and loving dedication to you.

Take your time to feel into this Presence. You may easily feel a connection — or you may feel nothing. Just be open, allowing and content with whatever you experience.

Imagine this Presence anticipates everything you need — and delights in supplying it, the moment the desire is realized.

Imagine what it would be like to be completely cared for with no strings attached, no needing to wait, no questioning of your wants in any way.

What would that feel like?

Imagine you or the infant feels hungry. And without question, this loving Presence provides the perfect food you or the baby needs.

For the baby, warm milk is provided. Perhaps you would like to hold them close and feed them? Or perhaps you prefer this Presence to do the honors — it's perfect either way.

And what about for you? What does your body most desire? What would give the most satisfying nourishment for your cells? Let it be given, let yourself enjoy it.

There is more than enough for you both. As much as you want. It's safe to eat, you are allowed to eat, and take as much time as you like. No one will take anything away until you have had your fill.

What kind of food do you most need right now? Let yourself be given, and become filled with the highest nourishment you desire. Love. Appreciation. Amazement. Gratitude. Courage. Fortitude. Joy. Wisdom. Kindness.

Whatever attributes come to you from this sweet Presence in this safe and lovely space, feel them flowing into you. Patience. Willingness. Trust. Benevolence.

You are being freely given whatever you most deeply desire — even those things you haven't always felt deserving of.

Let yourself be given and receive everything you would have wished for — but were too afraid to ask, let alone accept. Adoration. Thanksgiving. Robust health. Strength.

Feel yourself filled up with whatever is most nourishing, most satisfying. Savor it. Enjoy it.

And now — the infant is likely sweetly asleep. Perhaps you, also, would like to fall asleep. You are so warm, so content, so drowsy.

It's fine to simply slip into sleep... No one will disturb you; this Presence remains tenderly watching over you both. There is nothing you need to do; your only job is to remain present to this moment and do whatever feels best to you. No need to deny yourself anything. Let yourself sleep in complete comfort and trust.

Imagine yourself waking up. In your own time. Simply because you are ready to wake up. And that's perfect!

The world is ready for you to wake up, this beautiful place with this loving Presence as welcoming as ever. No urgency, no demands, no worries. Just this lovely, safe sanctuary where you can stay as long as you like, protected and cared for.

Eventually you may feel you have had enough. It's time for a little more stimulation! Your mind begins to think about your normal, everyday life. That's fine! After all, living in and exploring this wide world is why you are here.

You may want to leave the infant safely in this place, knowing they are continually watched over by this Presence. Or perhaps you would like to keep your infant with you, maybe tucked into your own heart.

Do what feels best. In your own time, you can return your attention to the outside world — but keep a sense of connection to this place of retreat. A place to regroup, to restore, to feel loved and cared for. A place where you are always met with welcome approval.

What was this exercise like for you? Was it difficult? Did you find yourself feeling uneasy or unworthy? Did you get distracted, irritated, or bored? Or were you able to relax and feel a sense of contentment for yourself?

We often have trouble allowing ourselves to simply be taken care of, to receive kindness, nourishment, safety from the world and those in it.

If you struggled with this exploration, here are a few questions to consider:

What makes it hard for you to care for yourself?
Do you believe you are good enough?
Deserving of care?
Worthy?

How easily can you allow yourself to receive whatever you want or need?

How generous are you with yourself? With others?

> *Because he is content with himself,*
> *He doesn't need others' approval.*
> *Because he accepts himself,*
> *The whole world accepts him.*[12]

Very early on, we begin to measure ourselves by external standards. By what others think we should do or be. By what society tells us is right or wrong. Unless we feel we measure up to these external standards, it may be a challenge to take it easy, to receive, to feel safe, loved, or nurtured. We have gotten so accustomed to measuring ourselves against some impossible standard of perfection, that we stopped accepting our basic goodness and worth.

Sitting in the practice of loving and giving to ourselves is a powerful act, no matter our age. Imagine if you loved yourself too much to accept others' negative projections. Imagine if you accepted yourself so completely, that no one's opinion could ever hurt you.

In a world that is swimming with criticism, approving of ourselves is a courageous and radical act.

---

[12] Lao-Tzu and Stephen Mitchell, "Chapter 30," in Tao Te Ching: A New English Version (New York, NY: HarperPerennial, 1988).

Remind Me — Why Are We Doing This?

"No problem can be solved from the same consciousness that created it."
(Albert Einstein)

You may wonder what these meditative exercises are all about. In the hardware/software biological metaphor, it's about moving away from the outer world/beta brain waves, and into the more spacious, intuitive alpha state of consciousness.

Remember that as our brains and nervous systems develop, they get trained into set patterns of neural pathways that become our automatic pilot of thinking/feeling/living. When we consciously access an alpha or even more spacious frequency of mind, it's like getting our hands on our creative control panel.

In these states, we can begin to reprogram our inner software, and start generating more positive, empowering pathways. Expanding them further through writing, art, movement, or any mindful out-in-the-world activity, encourages our automatic pilot to flow more easily into these kinder realizations, and create more beneficial experiences for ourselves and others.

Take a few minutes to think about what (if any) imaginings you may still retain from those early weeks and months of being in the world. Try not to judge whatever you perceive (if anything) as good or bad, nor do you need to go digging for deep, dark secrets. Just explore whatever you feel when you think about your first years of life. All babies and young children will experience some hurts, but it's how those experiences were interpreted and laid down that affects us going forward.

Often when we have some feeling of limitation or pain that doesn't seem related to anything, it can be harkening to a moment before we had language. Before we could name any experience, even as the energy of it slid right into our nervous system and began to broadcast a particular interpretation of life.

Perhaps that was the moment when Mother was taking a shower or Dad was distracted on the phone. Or they were having a terrible fight. Or just too exhausted to get out of bed and pick you up. So many reasons our early needs couldn't be met in the moment, so many parents who want to be there, but don't have their own resources to do it.

Here is an interesting question: *What kinds of conclusions about life or yourself or others, do you think you may have drawn from your very earliest days?*

Discovering a Gap That Wasn't

Perhaps you have heard some stories about your early days, months, or years that sound difficult. But it's a worthwhile consideration that some of the things you may assume caused you harm, actually didn't. Sometimes the experience wasn't perceived as frightening or lonely and caused no negative repercussions at all.

What have you heard about your first year on the planet? Were there circumstances you know happened that you assume caused you angst? Is your interpretation coming from felt memories, or based on stories others have told you?

What if you have been projecting painful impacts that weren't your actual experience in those moments long ago?

In one of my classes, we were exploring a very early, pre-verbal experiential memory. Due to serious illness, one of the participants had had to spend several months in the hospital during his first year of life. His parents lived far away and weren't able to make the long drive every day due to work and commitments at home.

Now long grown and far down the road of raising his own children, the thought of his infant experience brought sadness. He imagined himself as a small baby alone, cared for by doctors and nurses in a sterile, impersonal environment. He imagined feeling forsaken — not because anyone was deliberately cruel, but because those were the circumstances he had to endure at a time when he was most helpless.

But then he closed his eyes, relaxed his body, and went into a more meditative frame of mind. When he allowed his deeper intuition and memory sense to go back, he had a very different experience. Rather than feeling the painful loneliness he had projected onto that time, instead he moved into a space of peace and rest.

Gone was any sense of isolation. In its place was an atmosphere of quiet, safety, and contentment. He was amazed to recognize that what he had projected as a painful gap was actually a time of nurturing.

This discovery completely transformed an experience he had assumed was harsh and lonely. Now came the realization he had never felt alone, never felt abandoned. Where once he had told himself a story of separation and vulnerability, the more deeply remembered experience was one of safety and protection.

This is something to consider. During our earliest, pre-verbal days, our brains simply aren't interpreting what is happening in the same way adults do. And while an infant's brain and consciousness will certainly receive and absorb negative stimuli and retain impressions within their little nervous systems, the vibrational foundation of this tiny being is still highly connected to the beyond-time-and-space realms from which we came.

For sick or premature infants, a quiet, protected environment where their bodies are given the necessary support may be just right. Like an extended time in the womb, this is the space to delta-dream a little longer before they are ready and fully able to enter the world.

And for us now? When we go into a deep sleep at night, where do we go? We are still alive; we breathe, our hearts beat, but we are totally disconnected from the outer world — and we don't miss it. Nor do we remember where we went once we awaken. While we may remember some of our dreams, in our deepest sleep we willingly go behind a curtain that simply isn't available during our waking hours.

An Inherent Protection?

I have almost no memories before the age of seven. While I can't definitively know why, here's a conjecture: My early years included some major losses that undoubtedly impacted my parents and, consequently, me.

Scientists are hypothesizing that when faced with traumatic stress, our brains can activate a different pathway to store or suppress memories.[13] Could it be my defense mechanisms created a kind of amnesia as the way to protect my inner stability through those experiences?

On my third birthday, Mom gave birth to my baby brother, Stuart. We were now living in England, in a cottage outside of London by a golf course. Given her traumatic history with my birth and the distance to the hospital, the doctor wanted to pre-schedule the delivery. Since the due date was close, she decided it would be fun for us to share the same birthday.

She was admitted to the hospital, medicated into the twilight zone, and later emerged having borne a baby boy. Calling long distance from England to the US was a big deal back in 1960, but that evening they shared the wonderful news with their families, with relief and joy. All had gone well this time!

---

[13] Northwestern Medicine, "How the Brain Hides Traumatic Memories," Northwestern Medicine, accessed July 26, 2022, https://www.nm.org/healthbeat/medical-advances/how-the-brain-hides-traumatic-memories.

But then, after three months of being a healthy, happy baby, for no reason at all, he died. It was a warm spring Saturday and Stuart had been put outside for a nap in his pram. At some point he must have simply stopped breathing. When Mom thought it was time to get him up, she went over and called to him. There was no response. She wiggled his foot, again no response. Now alarmed, she picked him up. His body was lifeless.

Because it was the weekend, Dad was playing golf on the adjacent course. Somehow Mom got word to a nearby neighbor boy to go find him. Some sixty years later, Dad told me he remembered this boy running across the course yelling at the top of his lungs, "Your baby's dead! Your baby's dead!" Of course he rushed right home. Mom said that's the only time she ever saw Dad cry.

Because of Stuart's sudden death, there was an autopsy; but nothing was found, so the cause was officially "crib death." He was cremated — Mom and Dad sitting in the viewing room, watching his little coffin disappear into a doorway in the wall — and that's the story. There was hardly any mention of him going forward, only a few pictures in an album of this chubby, alert little baby.

We moved to Pittsburgh and Mom got pregnant again, but suffered a miscarriage due to an incompetent cervix. Now close to forty, she became pregnant one more time. To prevent miscarriage, the doctor stitched up her cervix and the pregnancy proceeded normally. Until around the six-month time, when she became suddenly, violently ill and was diagnosed with a bowel obstruction.

Emergency surgery was necessary to save her life, but the operation triggered labor and shortly thereafter the baby — a boy — was born, alive. She heard him cry. But back then such a premature baby couldn't be maintained, and he died shortly thereafter. I don't know if she and Dad even named him, and I've never seen any certificate of his birth or further recognition of his brief existence.

When I became a mother, thinking of what she had gone through weighed heavily on me. I asked her once how she had gotten through all those tragedies, especially Stuart's death. She said yes, it was horrible. But one day after some time had passed, she and Dad went for a walk on the golf course and suddenly she began to feel that things would be all right again.

But then she had to go through it one more time. And once more again. After the last loss, Dad was transferred to Japan and with that move, they put the thought of more children behind them. And only after we arrived in Tokyo do I finally start to have some memories.

So often for our own survival, our young minds and nervous systems simply have to put all the things we cannot process into a room and close the door. They become a layer within us, like an onion, that gets covered over with other layers as we grow more fully into our lives.

One day years later, when we have sufficient space and maturity, that layer may become exposed. This early hidden timebomb, still ticking away, has been waiting all these years for us to finally notice, take out, and de-commission.

When buried pain and trauma begin to make their way into our awareness, it can feel dangerous and shocking. The child in us who lived through the experience will suddenly come back on board. All those old feelings of incapacity and helplessness once again rise up, often with mega doses of anger, resentment, shame, or grief. How do we deal with what feels completely overwhelming?

What the child in us doesn't realize is that we have grown up since those days. The situation, the environment, the people around us have long since changed — and so have we. Trusting in our own capacity to find personal transformation and growth through anything we have lived, is the first step.

Next, is the willingness to accept — or at least imagine accepting — our past pain or trauma as a pathway for our growth. This takes time and patience — and compassion. And then one day we find ourselves finally able to digest what had previously felt toxic. A deep hurt becomes one more transformative influence in becoming the wise, whole person we came here to be.

The Ever-Present Spaciousness

The soft overcomes the hard;
The gentle overcomes the rigid.
Everyone knows this is true,
But few can put it into practice.[14]

Sit comfortably and close your eyes. Turn your attention inward, into your body. Tune into whatever sensations or emotions you may be feeling right now.

Perhaps there's some unease, perhaps some fear, perhaps some trepidation, as you have read the words in this chapter and are wondering what skeletons may lurk in your closet of origins. Don't try to change anything you are experiencing, just be present to it.

Notice whatever sensations are happening in your body. As you notice, become more consciously attentive to them and what they feel like. Focusing your awareness upon the sensations, don't try to change anything. Accept them completely.

Expand yourself to be present within a completely safe and neutral space. Consciously sift through your awareness and regardless of what comes up, see if you can receive it with a sense of acceptance and allowing.

---

[14] Lao-Tzu, trans. Stephen Mitchell, "Chapter 78," in Tao Te Ching: A New English Version (New York, NY: HarperPerennial, 1988).

Try on this image: Imagine that you are a great womb — even if you don't relate to the female embodiment — that contains all of life. From the greatest wonders to the smallest inconsequence.

In its vastness, there is room for everything to arise, to be present, to have its own space.

If you notice physical sensations, give them space and acceptance.
If you notice emotions, hold them with expansive neutrality and allowance.
If your mind throws out thoughts, silently witness them, but without reaction.

See if you can hold whatever you are experiencing right now, without any judgment.

Simply make space for whatever your experience is bringing forward, second by second.

Feel your capacity to expand this neutral, accepting space.

You may find yourself feeling challenged — perhaps by sensations or emotions or thoughts that feel unacceptable. Rather than buying into the conflict, simply feel yourself expanding with more space.
Space for the conflict.
Space for the unacceptable.

Feel your ability to expand enough to hold and accept whatever wants to come forward, without the need to judge, suppress or deny.

Explore what it is like to make space for all emotions, all feelings, all thoughts, all experiences.

To reject nothing.

Continue to experiment with expanding spaciousness; with meeting your sensations, emotions, thoughts, whatever comes up, with neutral space.

Imagine if you could hold anything from your life within this neutral space of acceptance.

Other people.
Situations.
Experiences.
Memories.

Take your time... if things come up that feel impossible to accept, just be open to that feeling. Without judgment.

It's perfectly fine to feel there are parts of life that remain unacceptable. Just recognize that this is the opinion alive within you. Hold that in spaciousness, also.

Accept yourself in every aspect you are experiencing. The parts of you that feel capable and strong, the parts of you that feel small and insignificant. The parts that are angry or sad or vulnerable. The parts that are wise and powerful.

Every time you notice something new about yourself coming up, be open and expansively accepting of it.

Have fun with this! See how radically spacious you can be! Of things that have made you cringe! Of things you would never reveal to anyone!

Let whatever comes forward into the light of your awareness be included within this spaciousness. Explore just how much space and allowance you can have.

Continue to maintain your openness and be present to whatever you are experiencing — even if it seems to be far too much. Even if it seems to be nothing.

Hold the space. Explore your own capacity for being present and allowing.

If you are feeling pain, sadness, anger, or anything disturbing or uncomfortable, just focus on expanding your sense of spaciousness, your ability to hold and remain nonjudgmental.

When we judge anything as wrong or unacceptable, we are alienating part of our experience. We are saying something shouldn't be. We are living in an inner conflict.

So just for now, just for this experiment, see if you can expand into so much space that there is no conflict. That even the worst can be made room for.

Your mind likely is coming up with some exceptions. Surely not this? This certainly is wrong!

Make space for your mind's thoughts also. Don't agree or disagree, simply sit in equanimity, that is larger than any opinion.

Every time something comes up that you meet with resistance, expand the space. Expand the neutrality. Allow all to be present within you.

Can you simply sit in the immense scope of whatever you experience, whatever life unfolds, even if for only a few seconds? Holding everything within this great womb, this great cauldron of creation and expression?

You may not be able to hold onto this place for long...you may feel confusion; or you may keep getting attached to thoughts or feelings again and again.

Every time something comes up that you feel conflict or judgment about in any way, release your attachment to that emotion as well, and just include it within the space.

Give yourself to this exploration for as long as you feel able — even five minutes, even thirty seconds of space is something. The longer you practice this, the more able you will become to stay present.

If this feels impossible, don't worry. Our human mind and nervous system are primed to have opinions about life. About what needs to be improved. What we need to fight. What we cannot accept. What we are afraid of.

But for a bit, imagine space. Imagine allowing all. Not being disturbed by any of it. Imagine having the capacity to weather every storm and encompass any problem, simultaneously with the arising of a solution.

Imagine moving forward into your day, your activities, interactions, meetings, all the doings — but with this spacious consciousness underlying it all.

What would it be like to carry this forward, into the beta world?

When you are ready, open your eyes — but gently. Sit for a moment and look around your environment with soft eyes. Yes, you are going to return to the outer world, to your beta brain frequencies, to all the doings you have in front of you.

But see if you can bring forward just a bit more spaciousness, as you once again go out into the world.

Don't worry if you couldn't maintain this openness or found yourself disturbed during it. This can be challenging and takes patience — something we may not have received much of in our early days.

We were born to ultimately expand the world our parents outlined for us — but in order to expand, we have to recognize where we are still perceiving and believing in limitations.

Do you see some places where you have been restricted in possibilities? In discovering new solutions?

Try bringing a little more space to situations, relationships, even memories — and see what happens.

PART V

Figuring Out How to Live in the World

Discovering the This and the That

When my little grandson, Archer, was around eighteen months, I got to see what I must have overlooked or simply been too preoccupied to notice in my own children's growing years: how completely fascinated he was by — everything! Anything and everything was new. As seen through his fresh eyes, the world was exploding in diversity and his little brain was absorbing on turbo-speed.

For instance: the discovery of cars. Then types of cars (van, jeep, taxi). Then cars versus trucks, versus buses, versus motorcycles, versus bicycles. Then colors of all these different vehicles (red car, white truck, yellow school bus). Then connecting cars to people.

It was an exciting day when he looked out the window, pointed to my little Subaru, and said "Noni's blue car!"

Birds became differentiated into crows and eagles and seagulls. Clothes became shirts and pants and socks and slippers. Food became bananas and steak and quinoa and carrots. From carpet fuzz to leaves on trees, nothing was unimportant. Everything was worthy of being discovered, everything had a separate meaning.

You and I were like this, also. Propelled out of the fusional consciousness of the womb, it takes time for our brains and senses to gradually attune to the variety of thises and thats and the ever-finer distinctions in this world of infinite stuff.

Emerging from all these differentiations comes the most important one of all: ourselves. We are not mother; we are not father or brother or sister or the bird flying in the sky. We stand separate.

Yikes! It's powerful and daunting at the same time! We better figure out this life thing as fast as we can.

Creating the Survival Manual: The Theta State of Mind

When people see some things as beautiful,
Other things become ugly.
When people see some things as good,
Other things become bad.[15]

Between the ages of two to seven, a child's waking brain is operating primarily within the theta range of vibration. Unlike the fusional delta, theta is the frequency of differentiation and super-learning. The mind is wide open and receptive, immediately interprets what it takes in, and has excellent retention.

This is our conscious entrance into the school of life and our personal environment is the classroom. Our brains are like sponges, sucking in everything around us, taking it all in at face value, and using it as our basis for understanding the world.

The theta brain state also coincides with our growing independence. No longer totally helpless, we now have physical autonomy in the world. We can walk. Run. Climb.

---

[15] Lao-Tzu, trans. Stephen Mitchell, "Chapter 2," in Tao Te Ching: A New English Version (New York, NY: HarperPerennial, 1988).

Communicate. Containing us becomes extremely difficult. Our little bodies and minds are in sync: to explore and learn about the world as quickly as possible.

Have you spent time with a two- or three-year-old recently? They have a lot of energy! Constantly moving, exploring, investigating, talking, running, and climbing, they need constant supervision (so they don't kill themselves) as they gain knowledge of the world through direct experience.

What's behind this bursting energy and curiosity? After the dreamy infant state of acclimation, a two-year-old is now fully present to the world and all its contents. Everything is new and exciting, everything a mystery to explore. The world is their oyster — sort of.

For they are still small, still dependent, and still ignorant of the larger workings of the world. There is no point of reference by which to compare or judge. Assumptions of life and the world come via the familial programming already in place, now combined with actual life experiences.

Besides learning and exploring, the most crucial business of early childhood is to figure out how to survive. Children won't always live with Mom and Dad, so getting a handle on life is of prime importance, with high priority being physical survival.

We learned not to cross the street when there are cars. Or touch the hot stove or stick anything into a light socket. We learned it hurts to fall down and it's not good to push or bite someone else. We learned about pain and all manner of sensory experiences — noises, sights, smells, tastes, touches. It's a big job to learn how to survive in the world, and it has to be learned relatively quickly — otherwise our time on the planet may be very short!

The theta brain's task is to build up a survival manual, which is absorbed and laid down within the little nervous system. But while theta was how we laid down our first learnings, we lacked any sort of discrimination. Nothing was questioned; whatever was received, got absorbed, accepted, and interpreted as gospel truth. This is what life is, this is how life works. Period.

Written within the manual were our perceptions about life, the world, ourselves. Men and women. Fathers and mothers. Husbands and wives. About what we can do or have, and what we can't. What behavior is acceptable, and what isn't. What is appropriate, and what brings trouble.

Even before we enter an actual classroom, we have made unquestioned meaning about infinite aspects of life.

The young child's mind absorbs experiences at face value, stores the lessons, and carries them forward in time. As we grow and mature, some of our lessons may morph, but others remain locked in our brains and nervous systems, exactly as they were laid down.

Some of our assumptions encouraged us to expand in particular directions, but others caused us to short-circuit huge swaths of our self-expression; to stunt potentials that were not welcome.

As older children or adults, when we find ourselves repeatedly feeling any defeating emotion, likely we are tapping into some part of ourselves we long ago needed to suppress. Our boisterous enthusiasm or our angry upset. Our willful determination or our jealous lashing out. When an aspect of ourselves was expressed but not well received, a child will assume it has no place in the world — and bury it as deeply as possible.

It's ironic that we create our life lessons when we are most helpless and dependent, without the ability to rationally understand the larger picture. So many of the assumptions laid down in our survival manual served to limit us.

Yet consider that there is also kindness here. We are still so naïve. The pruning process may feel harsh, but for our roots to take hold, any ground is better than no ground. We acclimate to the world in which we find ourselves — the world we are born into — to create a foundation from which we can grow. Ultimately beyond.

Exploring the Theta State of Mind

Let's have a little fun. Let's give ourselves permission to step out of our beta mindset for a bit, and experience what it is like to be a young child discovering something for the first time. We adults get very superficial in sensory perceptions of our world; it's amazing how much we don't see, hear, smell, or notice anymore, even though it's right in front of us. But a child sees it. A child hears it. A child can hardly wait to touch and taste it.

A child sees the most minute and tiny things — like a piece of lint on the couch! A child is amazed and fascinated and completely immersed in what our jaded mind sees as mundane and inconsequential. To them, it's all new and exciting: one mystery after another, unfolding before their very eyes!

Once we were that child. We were amazed and excited and filled with wonder. Each new day meant the start of infinite adventures! We were innocent, pure, blank little slates, eager to be filled up.

What was that like? What could that feel like now?

Wherever you are, stop for a minute. Deliberately home in on one tiny aspect of your current experience (for me, it's the countertop my hand is resting on).

Close your eyes and move into the experience of that one thing. How it feels.

Rather than quickly generating words to describe it, just experience it.

Notice how you relate to it through your body.

Be entirely present to your experience of this one aspect.

Immerse yourself.

Now — sniff it. Without describing it in your mind, just be completely present to whatever your olfactory sense experiences.

Notice the feeling in your nostrils, the different aspects of smelling that you perceive.

Keep resisting the temptation to name anything, just remain present to the wordless sensory experience your nose is receiving.

Don't be surprised if this is difficult! In our fixation on identifying, labeling, and mentally describing everything, we lose touch with the purity of sensation, free from language.

You don't have to do this next part, but if you did, what would it taste like? Again, no words, just the feeling of it on your tongue, the encountering of its flavors — and if they are familiar, imagine you've never tasted them before.

Now — what about the texture of this thing; and not just on your tongue, but against your lips, your teeth, the inside of your cheek? Go through each interaction in complete, feeling detail.

If your eyes have been closed, now open them — and look at this thing. Really look, really see. Notice the depths, the surface, the variations, the patterns, the colors… notice everything as if it is for the first time. As if you have NEVER seen anything so amazing before. As if it is the most unique and interesting thing you have ever encountered.

Consider: Is there anything you could learn about this thing? Explore that. What could you do with it? What could it become, in your innocent mind? What could it represent? Or be just perfect for?

Let your mind come in with a whole set of new ideas, possibilities you've never thought of before — the wilder, the better!

Imagine this oh-so-fun thing in all its different potentials, its different manifestations as this and that, in your playing and experiments!

Take as much time as you like; have fun exploring and imagining. Be a child free of preconceptions, delighting in this thing.

Eventually, when you have gotten as much as you would like out of this experience, look around your environment.

Notice your surroundings — do they seem different in any way? Perhaps more vibrant or colorful?
Are you surprised at anything you see?

Just register whatever you notice. Whether the world seems even slightly different in some way. And if so, how do you feel about it? Perhaps you feel a bit more interested — or perhaps not.

Whatever your experience, don't judge it, or yourself. Children have absolutely no opinion on how things "OUGHT TO BE" so right now, try to refrain from thinking any "shoulds" — either about yourself or this little experiment.

Just look with a child's fresh eyes, hear with a child's fresh ears, touch with a child's fresh touch… and have some fun. However, you do it, is just perfect!

"You Should Know Better!"

Did you ever hear those words? Or perhaps say them yourself to someone? Along with "for your own good," these may be the four most confusing words a child can hear.

What a child knows about the world is not much! It's a blank canvas without boundaries or definitions, without concrete walls dividing the right from the wrong or the good from the bad.

A child doesn't understand things the way an adult does. They don't know that Mom and Dad have lives, concerns, and histories pre-dating their arrival. They don't know what is expected of them and what is not a good idea. They are living life moment by moment, and it's all a big experiment.

How each moment turns out will determine the kind of "knowing" they absorb. Their own temperament and individuality will influence how they adapt the learning, but no one comes in knowing about life on the planet. No one comes in "knowing better!"

Perhaps this dictate of "You should know better" carries some resonance for you. Perhaps you feel the weight of an inner guilt, even if it isn't tied to anything specific, that strikes a slightly sickening chord within you. How many times throughout history has it been repeated, despite its total irrelevance — because children truly don't know! They are still innocent of everything we adults assume is universal knowledge.

You may carry a hidden expectation that you should know better, and find it operating in certain areas of your life. The assumption that we don't know things that we SHOULD know can be a burden that overshadows our sense of self-confidence and power — both within ourselves and outside in the world.

The Randomness of Root Causes

Here's an example of how a "should" gets absorbed. When Dad comes home, he usually picks you up and gives you a big hug and kiss. But he had a bad day at work, an earlier argument with your mom, and is thinking about how much debt they are in. When he gets home, he is already an accident waiting to happen.

Sure enough, he walks in and trips over your toys — the ones you play with in the time between Mom picking you up at daycare after her work, and Dad arriving home for dinner. Mom would usually help you clean them up, but she got distracted by her best friend calling—who had just been diagnosed with cancer.

So, he trips. To you it looks funny to see your big Dad summersaulting through the air and you laugh. For him to hurt himself isn't something you have even considered in your short life.

But neither Mom nor Dad thinks it's funny. In fact Dad loses it, as all his pent-up frustration gets channeled into a rant about what a mess the house is. He also throws in a few choice words about you (likely words he received in his own childhood, that still linger subconsciously) — which you might not fully understand but recognize as not good. Maybe he yells at Mom too, their own unresolved differences blowing through any remaining control he had over himself.

Mom also is engaged and responding to his upset through the lens of her own conflicted feelings. As her mixture of indignation, guilt, anger, and worry is unleashed, she, too, loses control — and they enact their own personal drama openly in front of you.

Even if they both regain some control over themselves, the shock of the event and intensity of their emotions will linger, and you will feel their unhappiness radiating out for the rest of the evening.

What kind of assumptions would your wide-open, super-learning theta brain state absorb from this experience? And what would be transcribed directly into your survival manual as a result? To you, the whole painful experience revolved around something that you caused. You assume complete responsibility.

I hurt Dad, *I* made them mad, *I'm* lazy, *I* don't know how to take care of things, *I* must be careful, life is scary and unpredictable, this is serious business.

And yet to your hurting parents, the scattered toys were simply the catalyst unleashing their own unresolved inner conflicts. Their dramas were brewing below the surface long before Dad even came into the house! Although you assumed full responsibility and might still cringe at this memory, nothing that they were experiencing or expressing was really about you at all.

Sure, it's important we learn to live together respectfully, clean up after ourselves, and follow rules to keep society running smoothly — but that's not all we absorb. Assuming we are responsible for the troubles of our world and those in it, we become attuned to trying to keep others happy (and how we fall short in our efforts), rather than keeping our eyes on our own unfolding possibilities and desires.

We learn, and then try to do, what will keep our environment as smooth as possible. To make our caregivers happy. To please those we love and need. To try and fit our development and desires into a world far more complex than we realize.

Consequently, much of what we assume will be at our early expense. That nips inherent attributes or potentials in the bud. That will point us in the direction of what we lack, rather than what we can become. Few environments can fully nurture our vast but still untapped and unconscious possibilities. Few of us will fully accept ourselves as being good enough, simply as we are.

The Present Child Method, created by Dutch homeopath Janita Venema, offers a beautiful metaphor for our early humanhood.[16] We come in as pure little beings full of infinite seeds of potential, but none of them are yet visible or known. As we grow and develop, these little seeds of potential will begin to sprout and come forward. Some of these seeds will be met with encouragement, while others are received with disapproval, rejection or even violence. The seeds that are met with a positive response are the ones we grow; while those that don't find acceptance, we quickly bury — and put a big rock on top.

The emerging of the child's expression inevitably stimulates responses that will pare down or deny certain aspects of our wholeness. The parts the world encourages will survive and

---

[16] Janita Venema, trans. Jean Thompson, Presentchild: A Gift for You and Your Family (Haren: Homeolinks, 2012).

grow into our seen characteristics, while we lose touch with those attributes that were shunned or rejected.

By the time we are adults, even though our outer environment will be completely different and we have much more authority over our lives, most of us will continue to live and act within the framework of that old manual — until those buried desires and potentials once again seek to get our attention.

Only much later will we begin to hear their siren's song as life pushes us toward their rediscovery.

Uncovering What We Assumed Was True

What do you remember between the ages of two and seven? Perhaps you have some clear images, or perhaps not much. Maybe you remember lots of fun times playing wild and free — or maybe you remember feeling afraid or restricted.

Do any unpleasant memories stick out? While they may have been painful, they can be pivotal in discovering both long-lost gifts and faulty truths we took on about ourselves and life.

It's helpful to remember that none of us came into a static world where only happiness exists. Pain, disappointment, abandonment, loneliness, anger, violence as well as joy, delight, excitement, laughter, and playfulness — every child will experience the full spectrum of life, through the interplay of their expanding self with the particular people and situations in their environment.

Although my memories from before the age of seven are almost totally inaccessible, there is always a vague uneasiness in thinking back. My mother was scrupulous in creating photo albums, and I've spent many hours looking through them, trying to connect myself with that little girl. What was she feeling? All I get is blankness.

When children have to rein in certain aspects of themselves because the environment simply cannot allow them to flourish, all sorts of assumptions settle in. Large aspects of ourselves must go underground in the molding to what we assume is the real world. What we bury doesn't die, of course, but we do lose touch with it.

Childhood is a selection process where only certain parts of ourselves will have the opportunity to come forward — and by the end of it, we assume we know who we are. Meanwhile, vast tracks of potentials and possibilities still lie in wait underneath our surfaces.

This is the true Hero's journey that takes place long after childhood is behind. Each of us is called — however clearly we hear it — to sift through all we took on about life and begin to assess its ultimate validity for us. Our deeper purpose is to discover gifts and truths beyond what others taught; to discover the meaning inherent within our own precious life.

How do we begin to hear the call? We may feel uncomfortable or discontented with certain aspects of our life. We may notice repeating patterns within different situations or relationships that don't feel good. Although we may not be in conscious awareness of our beliefs, they will be projected or reflected to us in the outer world. Our lives will confront us with the limitations we took on board long ago — and often the confrontation will sting.

How we take up our task, how we approach the discovery and re-awakening of our unique gifts beyond those early assumptions, is an organic process. When we have absorbed a lot of negative beliefs about ourselves or life, we will often find our experiences and others around us reflecting these perspectives right back at us. A large amount of patience, compassion, and trust will be our best assistants in our excavation process.

Life As Our Mirror

Do you have the patience to wait
Till your mud settles and the water is clear?
Can you remain unmoving
Till the right action arises by itself?[17]

Here is something I began to notice for myself. During the years Dennis and I were raising our three daughters and I was pursuing my training in the healing arts, certain incongruous themes began to catch my attention.

I am hardly alone in this, but as a health practitioner, I felt a great responsibility to my clients. When someone didn't improve, it was devastating. I would lose sleep, agonizing as if I was the cause of their pain and therefore it was up to me to save them from it.

And then there were the guilty dreams. Not every night, but periodically I would have a dream in which I'd unthinkingly done something so horrible, that the connection between myself and Dennis would be destroyed forever.

It was never an intentional act, yet somehow something occurred — something I had done in all innocence — that could never be forgiven, and I would be forever excluded from

---

[17] Lao-Tzu, trans. Stephen Mitchell, "Chapter 15," in Tao Te Ching: A New English Version (New York, NY: HarperPerennial, 1988).

what felt like life itself. The dreams were so real, that waking up would bring tears of overwhelming relief.

But most incongruous of all was a short series of small accidents — like backing my car up too far and scraping the bumper on a curb. This was completely minor with no other vehicle involved, yet I was plunged into an abyss of guilt and fear. Again, like I had done something so horrible, it was unforgivable.

I was petrified to tell Dennis about it — as though I had committed a deadly sin. Clearly these feelings were unjustified, but they took me over in complete dread.

While I had kept the dreams to myself, the car scrape was a material demonstration — which he would inevitably discover. I was scared stiff to tell him; wished I could just run away and disappear forever, rather than face the outrage my mistake would elicit. He would be furious, berate me, cast me away...

I lived in agony, biding my time for the right moment to break this horrible news. And then finally, expecting the worst, I told him. His reaction? He acknowledged it, suggested I get it repaired, and that was it.

My relief was immense! As if I had barely escaped annihilation! The suffering I'd put myself through...

What was this enormous guilt and fear all about? Why did these small, random accidental events, usually done in complete innocence, make me feel I had committed the worst of crimes and would lose all I most cherished? This just didn't make sense.

It took more years and a deeper understanding of our human makeup before I finally had the courage to explore these particular inner demons. In a quiet, meditative state of mind, I invited in the feeling sensations and emotions that always accompanied those situations. As I was present to my body's energy, I asked a question and simply sat in it: What was behind this perception of ever-pending condemnation?

When we sit in an attitude of receptivity long enough, turning away from all the external distractions normally occupying our attention, gradually we tune into our own inner landscape. What's been unconscious can start to come forward. I sat, allowing the present thoughts to gradually settle down, until my body was quiet and my mind receptive.

Nothing needs to be forced, although it can be hard to simply remain present and open. To disengage from our mind chatter yet again, and return to an awareness of spacious receptivity.

When we sit in the blank slate of a question without an answer, something new can come forward. As I remained open, an echo came up from the distant past. I began to remember.

We were living in a suburban house outside of Pittsburgh and I must have been around five years old. Down in the basement, Mom had a bunch of knickknacks sitting on an old table, including this little blue-and-white china figurine of a man dressed in elegant nineteenth-century clothing. I was fascinated by this little guy — which Mom had warned me not to play with.

In retrospect, I wonder how important that figurine really was, having been relegated to the basement. Nevertheless, I absorbed that warning as cardinal law — even as the little statue so tempted me to pick it up. One day when I was down there by myself, I disobeyed her. I picked it up. And... dropped it! On the floor, the little man lay in several pieces.

I was horrified! Scared and ashamed and afraid of what Mom would do when she found out. She wouldn't love me anymore... stop talking to me...freeze me out... cast me away. So I hid the broken pieces, went upstairs, and didn't say a word.

The next few days were horrendous. Living with the threat of her finding it, the end of my world felt imminent. I could barely sleep, so afraid of what was going to happen, but also wanting to tell her, to confess my terrible deed. It was torture, waiting for the inevitable. Days kept going by in perpetual dread, waiting for that guillotine to fall — while Mom seemed to remain oblivious to my sin.

Finally, I couldn't stand it any longer. In tears I sobbed out what had happened, expecting no redemption. My life was about to end. Maybe it was my own extreme upset that moved her, but instead of getting mad, she seemed simply surprised. "Oh, Susie, it's okay," she said. And that, as far as I remember, was the end of it. But my terror remained.

Puzzle Pieces

My parents were loving and clearly took care of me, but there is that blankness over my early childhood. Did some things happen way back then that could have accounted for my terrible sense of fear and guilt?

No one ever talked about it, so I never thought about it, but... perhaps the loss... accidentally... of what would have been three more children...

This is speculation, but surely there were weeks and months where their grief would have superseded their availability to me, the child who survived. Who still remained vibrantly alive, even as each new longed-for child was suddenly ripped away. What would the atmosphere have been, in the aftermath of yet one more tragedy?

What explanation does a child make up when parents or caregivers suddenly withdraw the attention and affection their world depends on? As adults, we know about the effects of loss and grief, but a young child has no concept of this. All they would know is that those they love and need have suddenly gone cold. Have shuttered themselves away, leaving the child outside and alone.

What happened? It must be something they did.

A little child can't understand beyond their experiences; everything reflects back to them. The concept of outside or separate causation is beyond their ken.

Is this where the concept of original sin comes from? Of parents living their own dramas and their children assuming responsibility for their pain? Of course sometimes a child does do something and it's a valid connection between their action and the parents' response. But so much in our early years was beyond anyone's control, least of all ours. Yet that's not how we understood it. And click — the burden of guilt settles, once again, into the next generation.

When this memory and the subsequent understanding came forward, puzzle pieces fell into place. I began to understand why this tremendous fear and sense of guilt permeated my life. How through one random, unthinking action, I believed I could destroy my world and lose those I most loved.

Years after the fact, this illogical but pervasive energy was still affecting me and my life experience. Affecting my feelings of safety, ease, and connection. Keeping me from trusting myself and others since, at any time, I could unthinkingly cause their affection to disappear — even if it wasn't clear how.

Making this kind of discovery can be a huge shock. It can make you feel almost sick. Such an enormous gap, such a sad belief for a child to have taken on and still be in resonance with, so many years later.

When we see something like this within ourselves, what to do about it? How can we ever fill that gap, restore our wholeness, right the seeming wrong we took on about ourselves?

Elevating To Love — My Process

Now, many years later, I sit down. Close my eyes. Focus on my breath, quiet my mind. Begin to consider the source of my fear.

I brought forward the awful feeling of having done something wrong. Of feeling alone and abandoned. Sensations began to appear in my body. Tightness; difficulty breathing. Panic.

I remained sitting, eyes closed, open to whatever wanted to come forward: sensations within my body; emotional states; images and thoughts in my mind.

My stomach began to feel sick. My heartbeat picked up.

Suddenly an image appeared in my mind. A very little girl alone in her bedroom, sitting in the corner on the floor. Crying. Quietly.
Longing for someone to come, but knowing no one would. No one would ever come.

She would be on her own forever.

A feeling of deep shame began to bloom within my gut as I saw this lonely little girl, completely forlorn.

I saw my adult self enter into the room and sit on the bed nearby.

Witnessing her pain, but not yet reaching out.
Exploring within myself what feelings were coming up.
Deep shame, even self-disgust.
A feeling there was something so terribly wrong within me, so unlovable and unacceptable that it must be shut deep, deep down, far away from the world.
Something that must be forever hidden and paid penance for.

As me, the present Susan, felt these feelings, another memory came forward, from my teen years. Again, sobbing alone in my bedroom because I believed something that was arising within me — my own sexual feelings and desires — were wrong. Sinful. That this was a deep flaw for which I must atone.

Fast-forward to another memory. Being told by Dennis that we were going to leave New York City and move to his hometown of Vancouver. While every part of me was in silent protest, I felt helpless to do anything but acquiesce.

Memory after memory began to emerge of these moments where I couldn't honor aspects of myself or my desires. Where I abdicated sovereignty over parts of my life experience, because I felt too small and inconsequential — too unacceptable — to trust that my own desires and needs were justified and worthy. To own that my life had meaning and purpose, beyond what others named for me.

Somewhere a long time ago, I lost parts of my own authority. Others make the call, put forward their purpose, organize the world. I allow, make do with leftovers, act secondarily.

I saw a history of self-abdication. But I also saw that this was my own doing. Not because others were making me, but because I shaped it into being. Feeling I was fundamentally unworthy, I whittled down my will, thinking that would keep me safe and cared for in the world.

In my mind's eye, I was still sitting on the bed with the little girl alone in the corner. I knew my parents didn't mean to cause her such suffering, but I also knew they didn't have the capacity to be available; to assure her that she was good and worthy of love, just as she was.

I got down on the floor next to her. Put my hand on her little, shaking shoulder. She wasn't crying anymore but had a glassy look of determination in her eyes. "Stupid! Stupid!" she seemed to be muttering — about herself.

"Oh, Susie," I said. "You aren't stupid. I'm so sorry." I settled myself closer to her and put my arms around her. She was rigid, resisting. I stayed quiet, just holding her, my own insides roiling with ocean waves of grief. Just holding, just waiting, just allowing. There was no hurrying this.

Through the flow of lifetimes, eventually her little body began to soften and the tears started. Gently I lifted her into my lap and held her close.

"Mommy and Daddy can't come for awhile, sweetheart," I said softly, her hair against my cheek. "They love you very much, but something happened that has made them very sad — and it has nothing to do with you."

I waited, just breathing steadily as she began to slightly shake in my arms. I noticed what was happening in my body as well, as I held her. The sadness still moving through me but also something else. A slight sense of relief, of lightening. Of recognition.

And then — the rising of something else. A raw… heat began to build in my gut. Anger?

At the waste. At all the times I'd bought into this powerlessness. All the abdications, the abandonments of myself.

She remained in my lap, stirring slightly. Perhaps feeling my own sense of strength rising up.

"I'm here with you and I'm going to take care of you, no matter what, Susie," I said as a new determination flowed through me. "You are safe with me; we are together in this."

She was alert now, listening to me. And I wanted to tell her that this was hardly the end.

"There is a great life in front of you, Susie, and everything turns out really well. You are going to grow up, you are going to get to do all sorts of amazing things, you are going to have love and laughter and wonderful adventures and fulfilment in your life."

This heat, this fierceness blossoming inside my own body was new to me. She turned her head to look up at me. Her eyes — my eyes — gazing into mine, still unsure but willing to listen. To trust.

"Don't worry, my sweet girl. I'm staying right here with you no matter what."

She cuddled more deeply into my arms. I turned my attention to my heart area. I breathed loving compassion in and out. For her. For her loneliness, her sadness, her confusion. And for my own.

I continued to hold her, affirming her innocence, her rightness. She had never done anything wrong. It was never even about her at all.

The trembling in her little body was subsiding; gradually she settled, maybe even into sleep. Likewise, my own body felt relaxed yet powerful; capable of strength if needed, but for now content to sit in quiet peace.

An immensity of love for her, for myself, flowed forward. And gently but thoroughly, that whole chain of pain and shame simply crumpled away, dissolved, dispersed. Gone was both the remembered and the unremembered, the terror of believing that I was bad or unlovable or unforgiven. No longer did that frightened old song sing within.

After all these years, I had finally been restored to goodness. To recognizing myself as the source of love, simply in being myself.

Compassionate Toward Ourselves

When we recognize these hurting places, what we need most is compassion. For ourselves. And possibly later, for those who deliberately or inadvertently inspired those alienating feelings within us.

Compassion for our confusion, our misunderstandings, our mistakenness. For how we took on others' pain and made ourselves responsible for it. And then finding the love for ourselves, which, when we open to it, is large enough to span any distance and heal our deepest wounds.

We have to take our time in this work. We have to allow our bodies and minds in all aspects — physiologically, neurologically, chemically, emotionally, energetically — to find a new coherence. So that which has long been operating underneath the surface, can come to light; be fully felt, embraced, released, and then encompassed within our expanded wholeness.

We don't just do this once and solve everything. It's as if the strands of our very DNA, forever entwining, will continue to throw up those darker shadows, those defensive/offensive programs embedded in our human blueprint — often with good cause.

Because people do cause harm, children do suffer brutality, wounds can be physical and psychological. Without the inborn ability to adapt and compensate, how many of us would even make it through childhood?

Our early days set up the playing field against powerful opponents. Only later will we finally own the ball. Only later can we start to question the rules, and eventually create a much more satisfying game.

Trust that no matter how difficult, you came fully capable of the challenge.

Life will throw up experiences that can send us back down those dark corridors — as that is where our restoration, our elevation, lies. We aren't here to stay divided. Any place we cannot accept within ourselves, or any evil we continue to project onto others, is an irritation we keep scratching until we finally look to heal the cause.

We did lose a lot, we have suffered. Sometimes simply recognizing and accepting that can be the first step in loving self-repair. Feel tenderness for yourself. Honor the pain; it was real.

Now consider that despite whatever happened in your beginnings, your destiny was never to stay small or broken. None of us came to be throwaways. Each of us remains ever pregnant with further potentials and possibilities.

Your wounds are ripe for healing. For restoring. For transforming.

What would it be like to lovingly embrace your past pain? What would it be like to let others off the hook?

Imagine moving beyond the shackles of your family and societal history. Imagine accepting yourself as whole. As good. As worthy. As love.

Now — if this sounds pie-in-the-sky, don't just throw up your hands in despair. Remember your wiring. It takes time to develop those new neural pathways, to divert the synaptic jumps into a more fulfilling reality. Consciously transforming assumptions rooted in pain is the greater work of our lives.

Find times when you are relaxed and deliberately start to imagine or strengthen your wiring to go into new, more loving, and positive directions. It takes time to build those circuits and reinforce them, so keep practicing. Your life is worth it!

Read these words and notice whether they resonate:

Your foundation was set up through people who were dealing with their own dramas or pain; they gave you all they were capable of giving. Your life has its own unique purpose and meaning. Use what doesn't feel good as your impetus for transformation and growth.

Questioning What We Know

Not knowing is true knowledge.
Presuming to know is a disease.
First realize that you are sick;
Then you can move towards health. [18]

As you prepare yourself for this exploration, consider this verse from the *Tao Te Ching*. For the moment, stand the idea of "knowing" something right on its head. Suspend — just for a moment — your knowings and see what that's like.

When you have some quiet time and space, sit comfortably and close your eyes. You may have lots of thoughts in your mind right now. Reading this chapter may have triggered some memories or questions, so it may take a little time for them to settle down.

As we have done before, an easy way to focus yourself and disengage from random thoughts is to pay attention to your breath. To your breathing.
To the in of the inhale.
To the out of the exhale.
Notice where the breath goes as you inhale.
How deeply does it move into your body?
How long is it?
How does it feel?
What is the quality of your breath?

---

[18] Lao-Tzu, trans. Stephen Mitchell, "Chapter 71," in Tao Te Ching: A New English Version (New York, NY: HarperPerennial, 1988).

And the exhale — what is it like? How long is it?

Keeping your full attention on your breath, invite the inhale to move more deeply into your body. You don't necessarily need to increase the length of time of the inhale, but gently invite it in more deeply.
And at the same time, slightly increase the length of your exhale.

Keep inviting the breath comfortably in a little deeper, and slightly increasing the length of your exhales.
If you can, reach toward having your exhales be twice the length of your inhales — but if that's too much of a stretch, then just find a rhythm that's comfortable and stay with it, counting (if you like) the length of your inhales and then the exhales.

Once you are feeling relaxed and focused, you can ask yourself if there is anything you would like to explore and shift, around the idea of knowing.
Of wondering whether you know enough.
Of being adequate in your knowing.
Of knowing what is right and what is wrong.
Of knowing something different about something you have assumed was true.

How do you relate to the need to know, in your life?

Notice what comes up. How you feel in your body when you question whether you know something or don't know something you think you should.
Follow the sensations, the feelings, without judgment. Just observe and be present to them.

And now: What would it be like to not know?

For this moment, imagine you don't know. That you have a blank space. A beautiful emptiness.

Imagine that you don't need to know. That there is nothing you need to know.

About yourself. About others.

If you are a person who has very strong opinions, who truly knows you know what's the absolute right way to do or be — or how the world should be — this may feel confrontational.

What do you mean, I don't know? Try not to get too affronted here; it's just an exploration, you can return to all your knowings in a few minutes. No one is saying that you don't know; there is nothing to defend against here.

Just experiment, for a few minutes, with what it's like not to know. And not to need to know.

Imagine all the knowings that have been crowded into your mind over the course of your lifetime.

Do any images come to you? Just be present to them.

Imagine all the knowings you constantly try to secure – how something should be done. How a situation should turn out.

All the lessons, all the dictates, all the shoulds and shouldn'ts, all the beliefs you have, all the book learnings and newspaper articles and absorbed understandings, all the rules and laws and customs, all the many knowings that you have acquired and come to believe as truth that pertains to you... to others... to societies... to countries... governments... organizations... partnerships... parents and children... siblings...

The amount of knowing within your brain is huge!

Get a sense of these knowings.
How do they feel to you?
Are they heavy or light?
Joyful or burdensome?
Are some knowings more important to you than others? Are some absolutely sacrosanct, so that to even question them feels like blasphemy?

Just notice. Don't judge anything you are experiencing, simply become aware.
Become aware of how it feels within you to have all these knowings.
Do some of them feel different than others?
Are some of them more natural or do some of them feel restrictive?

Do any of them seem to focus or be held in a particular part of your body?

Notice if there are any individual knowings that you feel are really and truly TRUE.
That you hold as gospel.
Take one out from the pile and look at it.
How do you feel about this knowing?
About what you know about the knowing?

Do you have any judgments about this knowing?

How does it contribute to your experience in life?
How does it affect your relationship with others?
How does it affect your self-concept?
How does it affect your work — or your leisure time?

Ask yourself how this knowing impacts your relationships with other people.
Does it ever separate you from others?
Cause you to hold others as wrong?
Or superior?
Does it ever make you feel wrong?
Or put any kind of barrier between you and them?

Just look at this; don't get too involved, other than sitting in the question and seeing what you notice.

For fun — and this is strictly for fun, you don't have to do it if you don't want to — imagine one of the knowings you feel quite attached to, doesn't exist.
That you don't know anything about it.

That you have absolutely no opinion on this subject at all. That you feel completely neutral toward the whole thing. That there is no judgment one way or another within you, on this.

Take some time here. It can seem impossible, so don't push yourself to where you can't go — but just imagine IF. IF you didn't even know this at all. IF you had no opinion or even awareness about it.

What would it change for you?
How would it affect your life, your experience, and your relationships?
How would it affect how you saw others, or what you expected of them?
How would it affect what you expected of yourself?

Not knowing is true knowing; presuming to know is a disease. Imagine if you simply erased your knowing, and it no longer took up any space within you.

How would you feel?
How would it change your life?

Just for fun, notice if certain aspects of your life would feel better. Or freer.

Are there ways that this knowing has actually hampered or constricted you in any way?
Not that we want you to go out and start robbing banks or shooting people you don't like — clearly this isn't about anarchy or breaking necessary laws — but it IS about questioning those knowings that restrict or limit you.
That restrain your fulfilment or free expression.
That tarnish your appreciation of yourself or others.
That keep you from experiencing more of life's goodness and satisfaction.

Has your knowing placed a restraint over your ability to fully flow with life?
With yourself?
With others?
Has your knowing caused you to criticize or condemn things that you would actually rather feel a sense of peace around?

The lines of the verse say, "first realize you are sick — then you can move towards health."
Perhaps there are some knowings that you absorbed from long ago that no longer serve your highest good.
That no long serve the highest good of others, or even of the world.
What would it feel like to live free of that yoke of knowing?
Free of opinions that straitjacket you and keep you from your own deeper wisdom?

Sit in the imagination of it.

Allow yourself to vibrate to a frequency where that knowing is no longer influencing you.

Find a frequency free of that restriction, where you create a different kind of experience.
To not know.
To just explore, to experiment.
To accept others in their freedom.
To accept yourself as already whole.

Sit with this as long as you are comfortable. When you start getting distracted or need to return to your outer life, see if you can bring an aspect of this new awareness with you.

If there are some old knowings you want to keep dismantled, be on the lookout. When you notice yourself falling back into that old pattern of knowing, catch yourself — and then deliberately disengage from it. Often it will be so automatic, you won't notice until you are quite far down the path of the belief; but bit by bit, you will get faster at recognizing it, faster at deconstructing your automatic responses and eventually realize you have a new openness to life. To others. To yourself.

How does that feel?

PART VI

Our Beliefs — Out in the World

Once we get beyond the age of seven, the basics of our manual regarding life on earth have been laid down and stored within our subconscious. Starting around this time, our brains begin to shift from a predominantly theta frequency into more beta: outward-oriented, judgmental, focused on solving problems. What we absorbed in theta, now gets implemented in the world through beta.

Our subconscious beliefs and lessons become the filter through which we perceive and act out in the world. Regardless of how true or helpful our conclusions were, they become our auto-drive, guiding us in our behaviors, reactions, thoughts, judgments, and decisions.

Perception is a creative force. Do you remember how our thoughts and emotions express energy? This energy affects our mood, our bodies. It affects our relationships and interactions. It flavors our moment-to-moment experience.

Those tricky hidden beliefs, perceptions, and expectations are like a director behind the scenes, influencing how we interpret whatever will appear on the stage of our lives.

As long as we remain unconscious of both the hidden assumptions and their guiding influence, they will continue to be repeated. Or to put it another way, reflected back to us, for better AND FOR WORSE. Many of the lessons we absorbed aren't even true! As we mature, many of them serve to stunt our growth and keep us in a holding pattern.

So many of our assumptions were based on what would keep us loved and safe — or simply alive — at a stage where we had no tools to question their validity, let alone imagine other possibilities for ourselves. We learned about life in our fishbowl, and then assumed our learnings were universal. The world we have defined is the world that is. Period. The self we have defined, through information gathered when we were at our smallest, most vulnerable and incapable, becomes our assumed structure.

Although we never stop growing and developing, parts of that structure remain frozen in time — still projecting those old, restrictive beliefs into our life experience.

When Expectations Collide

In our early months of marriage, when I was about six months pregnant, Dennis and I had our first major clash. It was a Saturday morning; I was lounging on the couch in my bathrobe, relishing an unstructured weekend ahead.

Dennis walked authoritatively down the stairs and told me in no uncertain terms that we were going into his office. It was time to prepare the annual newsletter for an environmental organization in British Columbia that he had founded.

This caught me completely by surprise. In fact I didn't even hear exactly what he was saying, being so distracted by the energy in his voice: demanding. Insistent. Even aggressive.

Instinctively, I drew back in protest — and suddenly the world blew up. From zero to one hundred, he became furious: accusing me of being selfish, how it was hardly anything to ask, how even his secretary hadn't minded helping him all these years, etc. etc. While I remained speechless and in shock on the couch.

I tried to defend myself, feeling my own anger coming up, which only made everything escalate. Finally he stormed out of the house to do the whole damn thing himself, while I remained on the couch in tears, thinking what a mistake this marriage had been.

It took a few painful days of silence and confusion, but eventually we both returned to our more rational minds, apologized, and moved on. But what exactly was that all about? How did that even happen?

I like to think that had it been reasonably presented (i.e., with advance notice and as a request), I would have been happy to help. It could have been a team effort followed by dinner out afterward. But that's not how it went down.

A voice raised in demand feels like a slap across the face to me — especially when it comes out of the blue for reasons I cannot, in the moment, understand. As for being called selfish? When I work so hard to comply, to go along with the program, to be easy-going?

Just when I thought it was safe to finally let down my guard and relax! Instantly all the subconscious memories of being a shocked, frightened, and isolated child caught in the middle of some adult crisis flooded through me, overwhelming my nervous system.

And for Dennis? In the years since, here's what I have come to know about his earliest days.

He was the firstborn to young parents married right after World War II. Five sisters followed him, and although the dynamics of such a large family surely contributed, his neural pathways were likely influenced from his very earliest life experiences.

He was born with club feet, and during his first year spent months in the hospital, receiving whatever the current, probably painful, treatments were. When he finally did come home, his parents would massage and manipulate his feet every day— and it hurt. As a toddler, he wore special shoes 24/7 that were connected with a splint — hindering his freedom and forcibly maintaining what would have been a painful reality for a very young child.

The good news is that all of this paid off, as his feet gradually assumed normal proportions and he has had no issues with them since. But what would he have decided about life, as those painful manipulations were forced on him daily by his own parents? What was his takeaway from having to cope with physical pain, separation, resistance, and restriction right from the start?

Perhaps one result is his extremely high pain threshold; what would be agonizing for another, he barely notices. He also has a keen eye for faults and will work tirelessly to improve something he believes is wrong, often against great resistance. He has high expectations of himself (and others) and has trouble feeling satisfied until things have been completed to his gold standard.

As with his feet, this hard work and dedication to excellence have paid off both personally and environmentally — he has been a driving force behind protecting and creating ongoing stewardship for large areas of BC's wilderness.

Because his visions have been so large, and often mean going against institutional status quo, he inevitably needs the support of others to bring them to fruition. And here is where those early assumptions can work against him. Life was full of immense resistance from his very beginnings and so immense resistance is automatically expected — even when it might not have to be there.

One of his life challenges has been learning to temper his approach from one of urgent forcing, to inviting collaboration. When he approaches others in a receptive, more relaxed way, his natural leadership shines — but when he goes in with a sledgehammer, things can backfire. Certainly that was my reaction, when his unexpected request came across as an insistent demand I had no choice about.

That Saturday, our inner stories went online — and the systems crashed! Shocked and betrayed by the one person we hoped would always see things our way, we found ourselves disappointed yet again.

Knowing for Others

Can you think of a time when you got into something with someone you care about? Our greatest disappointments can come when those unconscious judgments, beliefs, and expectations aren't agreed with by those we love.

While painful, the mirroring of our own misunderstandings can be the first step in freeing ourselves from their bondage. If we can use these moments to go deeper within ourselves and tease out our unconscious assumptions, they become opportunities for our own evolution. Once we become aware of our beliefs, then we can consciously move toward creating a more benevolent reality.

Here is something to consider: If you didn't have any ideas or judgments around something, would you be bothered if someone else exhibits it? If you hadn't created a concept around a particular label or way of being, if you had no judgments or felt threatened in any way, would you feel any discomfort?

When we have learned early on to see something as "wrong," it becomes a susceptibility we are unconsciously always looking around for. We appreciate others who agree with our beliefs and recoil from those who don't. Any hint of it within us is denied, and anyone else who expresses it, must be shunned.

We have an antenna constantly scanning the environment — and when it picks up that signal, we rise up in reaction.

If we were taught to suppress certain traits or behaviors within ourselves, then we cannot tolerate them in others.

When we see someone who appears to embody that trait, we don't like them. If we ever catch a whiff of it in ourselves, it's quickly repressed. Either way, we are caught; unable to tolerate or reconcile certain aspects of our experience. Unless life completely conforms to our demands, we cannot feel at peace.

Think about someone you have felt antipathy toward. Interesting word, "anti-pathy." The opposite of sympathy. The *Oxford English Dictionary* defines it as a "deep-seated feeling of dislike; aversion."

Does anyone come to mind?

If it's a stranger, ask yourself what it is that you find unattractive. Simply direct the question toward your mind, and see what comes up. Is it something about the way they look? How they talk? What they say or do? Do they remind you of someone?

If you remain enquiring, you may discover a whole story behind your antipathy. Explore it. Be like a detective toward your own thoughts and judgments about others. Become curious about what turns you off, and the deeper reasons or imaginings behind it.

Although you may not be clued in immediately, see what kind of associations you are making — and whether any of them stem from your childhood.

Of course things get really challenging when someone we love or regularly interact with pushes our susceptibility buttons. How many of us go crazy over how a family member chews their food… or ties their shoes… or looks after their possessions. These tend to be smaller things but can nevertheless build up, especially when it's regarding something we believe deeply in.

Moving Beyond a Limiting Judgment

What if you do regularly interact with someone who exhibits inappropriate behavior? What if it's your boss or co-worker? Or your neighbor? What if it's your PARTNER? Or your child (that's easy, you just keep correcting them until they come to see it your way!) Or your best friend's partner? Or your in-law?

Being around someone who continually pushes our buttons can be so stressful, we can actually become ill. When we either can't or won't remove ourselves from the relationship, then we have to make a choice. We either continue perpetuating our own suffering, or consciously choose to become so supremely self-loving, that we are willing to use this for our own growth.

If you would like to experiment with finding a new place from which to relate, this exercise is for you.

*First caveat: if you are being affected by someone who is abusive or destructive or causing literal harm, then the first step is to find support and create a plan to remove yourself physically from them. Anyone who is in so much pain that they can't help inflicting pain on themselves or others, must be stepped away from. Self-love means working from a place of safety first and foremost.

Second caveat: Start with something small — a person or behavior that doesn't cause extreme reactions within you. Don't demand more of yourself than you will be able to shift.

Think of someone who bothers you. Perhaps it is someone quite separate from your day-to-day existence, or perhaps it's someone closer — like someone you live or work with who does something you dislike.

Once you have found this bothersome person or behavior, sit comfortably and close your eyes. Turn your attention inward.

Get quite focused on what bothers you. Picture or experience it clearly in your mind's eye.

Notice whatever you are feeling in your body. What kind of sensations are happening? Don't change anything, just become aware of the sensations and activity in your body, as you contemplate this bothersome thing.

Notice your emotions. What words would you use to describe them? Explore them, let them get filled out in your awareness. Feel the emotions in full Technicolor.

Next, investigate the connections between your emotions and the physical sensations you may be experiencing.

What's the physical sensation of anger, for example?
Or frustration?
Or irritation?
Or fear?
Hatred?
Remain present to the emotions and the sensations, even as you clarify them further with your awareness.

Don't try to fix anything, simply investigate what happens within you — your body, your body chemistry, physical sensations, emotions — around this particular dynamic.

Notice what your thoughts might be saying. Again, don't try to change them; just notice the thought-energy your mind automatically projects when experiencing whatever this person instigates within you.

Without buying into the thoughts, dig deeper into what your mind is saying about this person.

What kind of judgments is your mind making?
What is your mind fixated on, regarding this person or behavior or experience?

Even though your mind, body, and emotions are very involved in this, try to enlarge the space around the whole experience so that part of you remains unattached. Try to see it from a larger, neutral perspective.

Imagine you are a scientist investigating this phenomenon. Remain detached as you observe all that is happening within you.
This isn't easy, so don't be surprised if it feels impossible to retain some neutrality — but try to stay with it.

Be present to the emotions within you, as your mind is making its statements about this person or behavior. Don't suppress any emotions. Go ahead and let them express and expand as much as they want, even as part of you remains detached and observant.

Be open, aware, and allowing of your emotions — as well as of any physical sensations.

Investigate what your mind is saying, as it lectures about how this person or thing is wrong. Retain your more spacious perspective, even as you are fully present to your habitual energy around this.

If you notice you've gotten swallowed up by the old story, deliberately step back into neutral observance.

You may discover that your initial judgment has deeper layers.

Be present to the judgments. What stands behind them?

For instance, if you judge someone as arrogant; or selfish; or annoying in any way, what else do you assume about them? You may discover a whole background story behind that initial word or judgment. You may discover you have assumptions — maybe a whole storehouse of them — that go beyond your actual experience of this person.

Keep reaching for more clarity and understanding about what this bothersome behavior, this "is-ness," actually represents to you.

As you stay in this neutral observation, still completely present to your physical sensations, your emotions, your judgements, go back in your mind's eye through your life... into your childhood, long ago.

Have you had these feelings before? Is there a connection between this current experience, and something from your history?

Does this experience have an older resonance for you?

Keep moving back, keep sifting through the strands of your memory and feelings to see if there are deeper connections to be made.

Were there experiences that gave you a particular belief about the qualities or characteristics or actions that currently disturb you? Did you hear other people making judgments? In what context? In what circumstances?

This isn't about good or bad, right or wrong, so if you keep getting hung up on "But it's just WRONG!" try to stay neutral. Maybe in your family of origin or adult perspective, it IS wrong — but in theirs, it was a survival strategy. A coping mechanism. A justifiable interpretation of their environment.

Consider that this exploration is about creating new options of experience for YOU — beyond just antipathy. Where you can feel at ease, even in a world where people or qualities like this exist.

Perhaps you will get a clearer understanding of where your antipathy developed, but perhaps you won't. There aren't necessarily "ah ha!" answers, but consciously witnessing your experience creates more space for you, even in the face of that bothersome behavior.

Becoming conscious of our automatic responses and patterns gives us access to new possibilities of experience. You may never agree with or even like that person, but you can create more space and ease for yourself, regardless. Once we can access our own energy, we finally have the option to change it.

Here are some questions you can ask yourself, as you simply sit and observe your own process:

Is it possible they have no idea this bothers me?
Is it possible they mean me no harm?
Is it possible this actually has nothing to do with me?
Is it possible I am reminding them of someone, and they are projecting their confusion onto me?
Is it possible they are reminding me of someone, and I am projecting my confusion onto them?

Is it possible they are just doing the best they can, under the life circumstances they have known?

Is it okay that they are still working things out for themselves in their life's journey?

As you scroll through these questions, one or more may resonate within you. If you find one that does, just sit in the question(s), without looking for answers.

Immerse yourself in the question, applying it to the person, to their actions, to whatever you find most disturbing — but without the need to find a conclusion.

Be present to the question itself, as applied to them. Refrain from reaching for any answers. Just stay spacious and receptive to whatever you discover.

Remain focused without rushing or forcing anything to "happen," but simply be present to your own questioning mind and body, your own ever-evolving spirit, your own spacious heart.

When you feel you are ready to come to a natural closure (or it's time to move on), take a final moment to give thanks for whatever you experienced. Something in you will have shifted, however you perceived it.

Then gently open your eyes, return your attention to where you are, and move back into your present time and space.

This can feel very difficult, so try not to judge yourself or your experience. The last place we want to find "room for improvement" is within ourselves. It's always far easier to find things wrong with everyone/everything else "out there."

Sometimes the greatest act of self-love is to finally stop fighting against something we can't change, and instead encompass both sides of the equation. Find the common ground — within ourselves.

Below is a short wrap-up of steps you can take (which is by no means all-inclusive), which don't require participation from anyone else.

Quick Guide to Moving from "Wrong" to (at least) Neutral

First — thank yourself for being open to the possibility of change. It's not easy, it doesn't happen overnight, and you may always wrestle with this at some time or another, but never from the same place of complete unconsciousness. Acknowledge your growth, your generosity toward yourself, your courage. Be grateful that you are who you are!

Second — if the meditative processes we've explored in this book help, then put yourself in that meditative space and feel into the change you want to embody.

What does it feel like to have this different energy? Experience it within yourself. Within your body, your emotions. Within your cellular, neural structure. Envision the person or situation from this new perspective, where they are actually your kind friend, helping you evolve — and you are equally kind in return.

Third — keep reminding yourself of this new way of being, as you move through your life. You will definitely get caught in the old ways, but eventually you will catch yourself sooner. It takes time to empower a new network, so don't be too impatient with yourself. Just live from this new energy as much as you

can. When you fall back into the old, don't beat yourself up —
just shift back as soon as you are able.

Fourth — know that as you shift these old, less satisfying
patterns, you are changing not just yourself, but others as
well. You won't know how many people or situations will be
changed for the better by your intentions, but it is significant.
You are truly becoming the change that you seek in the world.

Fifth — be grateful for the message/messenger. If they hadn't
pointed out a place you were ripe for transforming, it might not
have happened. As long as we stay stuck in our own prejudices,
we can't discover the allies all around us. Anyone can be our
doorway into love.

If you close your mind in judgments
and traffic with desires,
Your heart will be troubled.
If you keep your mind from judging
and aren't led by the senses,
Your heart will find peace. [19]

---

[19] Lao-Tzu, trans. Stephen Mitchell, "Chapter 52," in Tao Te Ching: A New
English Version (New York, NY: HarperPerennial, 1988).

PART VII

Elevating to Love

Elevating With a Partner

We all have immense capacity to help and be helped by others. We are loving beings, and nothing is more loving than to be a completely present, nonjudgmental space for another — or allowing them to be that for us.

It's also a radical act, for most of us have been taught that we need professionals to be in charge of our healing process. This disempowers and denies the integrity we each possess. Knowing you and I are fully capable of transformation is transforming all by itself.

There are many ways we can assist each other. A degree isn't required — and opportunities can open up at surprising times! A dear friend and healer of great perception, Dr. Roland Guenther, has allowed me to share this story with you.

Dear Susan,

You write about perceived wrongs and traumas. Can I share a story about that with you?

Before Christmas, my dear wife Barb and I had a bad fight. I wanted a Christmas tree, Barb didn't. Not even a small one, not even when it is in my room, not even if I only put it in the garden. Why? Because Christmas was always extremely pain-ful in her family of origin. It was about obligations, lies, "you have to...," about getting a gift and later hearing that now you have to do something in return, and so on.

I understood that, but my own young part still wanted a Christmas tree.

The next day we settled. I got, and decorated, a very traditional Christmas tree for us both. Then we decided to have a glass bowl filled with sand from the beach, which I went and got, and a bucket of beach pebbles.

On Christmas Eve, we told stories of Christmas: everything that we remembered, all the bad things that happened, all the grief about what should have happened and did not, all the betrayal, the pretenses, the lies around Christmas. With every story we told each other, we held a stone in our hand. That stone stood for the memory of it. After we were done telling a story, we placed the stone in the bowl as a sacred offering of our pain on the Christmas table. In the end, we blessed it with a prayer and lit a candle in the midst of the stones.

It felt so good to include the dark side, the painful side, of our lives and give it a place in our celebration. I think we will make that a tradition. Healing always goes with including something that had to be excluded.

Coming together to honor past pain as the means for our transformation is a tender gift we can give ourselves and each other. When someone else honors the inherent value of our suffering, our recovery quickens. The internal war begins to subside and suddenly we discover that everything in our origins can be love in the making.

Laying Down a New History Through Love

Although my parents ended up with just me, it turned out to be practical because Dad's career moved us around a lot. Just when I would finally feel settled in a new home and community, "The Breakfast" would happen. Sitting at the table, Mom and Dad would look at each other, look at me, and say, 'Susie, we have something really exciting to tell you!"

And in no time, we would once again be packing up and moving on. In the first four years of my life, we lived in Rome, Geneva, and London. We went on to live in Tokyo, Rio de Janeiro, and Lima, with periodic stints in the USA. I finished high school in Miami and was going to Dartmouth College in New Hampshire, when my parents made their final move to Houston, Texas.

Through the constant outer changes, Mom remained the center of my universe. She organized our new homes, encouraged making new friends, was there when I got back from school. She was my anchor, and I was hers as we moved from one foreign environment to another.

My father, however, was a different story. While Mom and I were the home team, Dad had an outward life and wasn't around that much. He traveled a lot, worked late, and used weekends for socializing and sports. Seeing him was more the exception than the rule.

As I got older, he occasionally became more involved — but not in comfortable ways. I was a little afraid of him. He would show up when he thought he needed to teach me something, and it was never a good experience. I had confused feelings and usually did my best to stay out of his way.

Dad was the oldest of three sons, born to very young parents back in Willoughby, Ohio. His father's grandfather had created great wealth, most of which was now long gone. Although still fortunate, his parents had to make their way in the world with far less support than they might have expected.

His mother was artistic, dramatic, and passionate. She dreamed of being a renowned actress on the world stage, but instead settled for performing in amateur productions and being a wife and mother to three rambunctious boys. His father, a keen outdoorsman, created a small engineering firm in rural New Hampshire, and the family activities revolved around skiing, hiking, fishing, and hunting.

When Dad was eight, he got scarlet fever followed quickly by the measles. He didn't recover well and began losing weight. The illnesses had triggered Type 1 diabetes.

Insulin was only recently discovered, but Dad was lucky to be treated by the leading diabetic specialists of the day. He and his mother spent months in the hospital learning how to manage his condition, and for the rest of his life, survived by injecting just the right amount of insulin multiple times a day. The slightest discrepancy, if not rectified quickly, could send him into a coma and death.

His mother's (my grandmother Nona's) flare for the dramatic extended into anxiety, jealousy, and possessiveness. Although I don't know the details, his relationship with her became strained as he grew. He had an enthusiasm for all life could offer, and his disease probably fueled his ambitions — proving to himself and others that it was no hindrance.

The one thing diabetes did prevent him from doing was entering the armed forces during World War II. Unable to rise to the challenges of war, he rose to athletic heights in skiing, ski jumping, and mountaineering — which remained great passions throughout his life.

He also achieved academic heights, graduating as class valedictorian from Dartmouth College, and becoming a Rhodes scholar. He never allowed his illness to hold him back from anything — although there were some very close calls with death.

Multiple times he lost track of his insulin balance in some remote place — like a mountain ski hut or a foreign city — and was discovered by chance, stumbling around in confusion or already in a diabetic coma. Those who loved him, like his mother and mine, had to accept he would always live large — and pray he would never skate too close to the edge.

He exuded a kind of radiance, making friends around the world and ever interested in pushing the boundaries of adventure. Yet I never felt included in his radiant universe. Throughout my childhood, we were never close; and the times I felt included or appreciated by him were rare — usually in an alcohol-induced moment of over-affection, which was equally uncomfortable.

When I was at college, I began to feel quite angry with Dad. He was always distant; never easy or available to me, except to lecture or make me "better," but not in a way that felt loving. I even wrote him a letter describing my discomfort with our relationship. Unfortunately I mailed it, thinking he needed to understand how I felt. He never responded — but Mom did.

She sent back a sternly worded letter, expressing how hurt Dad had been by my words — which only piled guilt on top of my confusion.

After I married and was building my own family, we became closer. Dad adored Dennis and was a much more available grandfather than he had been as a father. My daughters loved him easily and he took great interest in their lives, talking and listening to them as I'd always hoped he would with me.

In his later years, he expressed his sweetness and affection to me without reserve. Gradual blindness and memory issues developed, but he never complained. As his world narrowed, his appreciation became more exuberant. During my frequent visits to Houston, Dad would hug me tight and exclaim, "What a daughter! What a daughter!"

But despite the close and loving relationship we ultimately experienced, those old, confused feelings around our earlier days didn't go away. I still had memories that felt unpleasant and similar feelings would echo in current scenarios with other people.

How to shift this? It clearly didn't need anything from him; this lived only in me.

Laying Down a New History — My Story

I sat down and closed my eyes with the full intention of laying down a new history — both for myself, and our history as father and daughter. Focusing within, I worked to still my mind until I sat in quiet spaciousness.

With my intention present, I remained open and receptive. Rather than directing anything, I invited the process to happen. As I sat, a memory began to surface.

We were living in Pittsburgh; I was about ten. School had started and I was having trouble with arithmetic. It was still warm and light in the evenings, so after dinner I would go outside to play with my friends until bedtime. But not this evening.

Dad sat me down at the dining room table and tried to get me to understand arithmetic — impatiently. I didn't want to be there, and he got more and more exasperated. He was far too close to me, overbearing and angry.

As I sat with the memory unfolding, my body began to contract, and my stomach tightened. I wanted to physically run away, but I couldn't move.

Across from where we were sitting, the front door was open to let in the cool air. Suddenly my friends came to the screen door and asked if I could play. Dad said loudly, "No! She has to stay here and learn her arithmetic!" Chagrined, they left — while I remained behind, trapped.

I felt like a bug pinned to a corkboard. Everything in me wanted to get away. Although he didn't lay a hand on me, I squirmed as if under his stern grasp, a prisoner desperate to escape.

The sense memory of the experience flooded through me. Physically shrinking, fear and tears, along with anger and resentment, but also something more unpleasant. A feeling of being forced, almost violated, against my will.

I sat open to everything I was experiencing, as if it were now. No trying to suppress, no trying to breathe anything away, allowing all my own discomfort and anguish to be as large as it needed to be. Making room for everything to come forward.

We've all done the avoiding, the repressing, the shutting away of our trauma or suffering, and often at the moment, that's the best way to survive. But now, years later, there was no need to keep anything locked up. It was time to let the ghosts come out into the light of a new day.

I stayed present to my body's sensations and emotions, to the rising and falling, the ebb and flow. Heat and cold, shaking and trembling, energy running itself through my body however it wanted to. I stayed open to it all.

It seemed to take forever… but finally, finally, the storm began to pass and, in its wake, calm. A space into which something new could emerge.

What would be a better reality for me to remember and energize?

Freed from the old energy, I contemplated different scenarios. What would be a more satisfying experience? I began to try some out.

Here was one with promise. We are at the table with the front door open and my friends appear. They ask me to come and play. I look at Dad — and now, instead of his curt former reply, he looks at the kids, looks at me, and smiles. "Sure Susie, go play with them. Have fun." Wow.

I sat in that experience, aware of everything happening in my body. That felt okay — in fact it felt pretty good. I waited, focusing on all the sensations and emotions within me as I stayed present to that scenario. There was definite relief happening within, a loosening of the muscles, a relaxing in my chest.

But gradually it felt as if there could be something even better, just waiting for me to discover…

Then I got it: While this scenario gave me my freedom, it didn't change the dynamic of our relationship. I wanted something that would bring us together. That embodied the closeness I longed to have — and ultimately did discover, far along in my adulthood.

How about if, instead of me resisting his teaching and impatient insistence, it was the complete opposite? What if I wanted to figure it out? And what if he enjoyed helping me?

What if this was something we could do together, like a team? Not him forcing while I cowered, but instead a father/daughter adventure we could share together.

I began to see a truly satisfying, mutual experience. He would have the pleasure of helping me grasp what I hadn't understood, and I would gain my own confidence through his encouraging tutelage.

Now I didn't even want to go play with my friends! I just wanted to spend that special time with Dad at the dining room table. I could even see him winking at me when my friends came to the door and I said, "Sorry guys, I'm working with my dad."

I sat with my eyes closed, envisioning and living this new scenario. Feeling it as real. Drinking it in, letting it settle in my gut, in my heart, spreading out with a warm radiance. Sweet and true. The teamwork between us, the closeness…

And then, as I continued to sit in awareness of this new reality, the truth of it came gently home. This actually was reality. This was the deeper truth, underlying any temporary blips in our greater life story as father and daughter.

My heart expanded. Anything that felt awkward or painful or confusing — throughout our whole lifetime together — just dropped away. And I knew: There was never really anything keeping us apart other than the weight of human detritus and confusion. I could finally stop perpetuating that old, painful story. A new reality had taken root.

Could I still return to that old story with its disturbing energy? Of course, but why? All the dross cluttering up my sense of safety and peace was now dissolved. Dad and I were aligned in this new truth, now reverberating throughout all our history together.

In our deepest heart, we don't want to feel anything other than love for those we care about — and yet so often we do. It may seem impossible, but often one adjustment, one movement away from the misunderstandings or harshness of a thoughtless moment can shift relationships both past and present.

To truly change our experience of a relationship, we must be flexible in how we see others and how we see ourselves. We can't find the best "true" story, until we are willing to believe in our shared ability to grow — even beyond the constraints of time and space.

Now — one thing that made this easier for me is that my dad and I had already changed in how we were relating. In shifting that old memory, I wasn't faced with ongoing, in-the-world contradictory experiences.

Could I have done this if our relationship was still distant or awkward? It surely would have been more difficult, and yet, if we dig deep enough, somewhere we will find a place of connection, of sweetness, of some positive characteristic we can grasp and say, "Yes! This is who you are!" Even if we have to move away from them, before we can settle into a more satisfying recognition.

The Transformation Process:

- First step: Be receptive to creating a new story. We have to be willing to disengage from our old interpretations
- On the path: Know that by moving beyond a perception of wrong, we can bring forward a more satisfying right.
- Destination: Realize that even our worst pain holds us in self-imposed shackles — as we discover a more expansive reality, we literally heal our past and those in it. We elevate all participants to love.
- Outcome: New freedom and joy, rippling through our life experience.

Love yourself enough to trust in your evolution; it's always there, one new possibility at a time.

Dad ski-racing, doing what he loved most ©

With Dad

Changing a Story: Discovering a Higher Truth

It's quite annoying others can't fix what feels broken inside us, even when they were the ones who did the breaking. It's so much easier to hold them responsible — for our pain, and/or the means to relieve it.

But that's not who we are, or why we are here. We always have the option to move beyond the limitations and dependencies we absorbed from others, and discover the ever-present ability to stand in our own worth.

How do you feel about your parents or the people who raised you? Are there people who hurt or harmed you? Who didn't give you the love and appreciation you would have liked? Who belittled you?

Here is an important question. If you could transform this, if you could free yourself from your pain, would you do it?

Think about this for a minute. There is something rewarding about holding someone else accountable for the wrongs. It's comfortable to justify our ongoing anger or resentment or even hatred. But it doesn't actually help us. In fact, it is a completely unloving act — and not just toward them.

Can you love yourself too much to remain in bondage any longer?

Perhaps you would like to rewrite a story from your past and begin to lay down a new, more satisfying history. As with so many other processes we have done together, you will need to access a different consciousness from where the "problem" currently resides.

The idea is to take an uncomfortable memory and literally rewrite it into our neurology — our body/mind/emotions — in a way that brings us some peace. Whether someone else was the instigator or we feel the fault was ours, the process is the same.

Go gently here. Follow what feels appropriate, and back away from anything that pushes you too far. Stay in your own comfort zone, even as you stretch the envelope just a little bit further.

If it feels too much to do on your own — and be honest with yourself — professional or personal support may be the better course of action. Seek out someone you trust who can be a loving, heart-centered space for you.

In whatever way you proceed, honor your life, your experiences, your potential to heal — and the right pathway will always open up.

Think of a memory you have from your early childhood. One that makes you feel... yucky. Perhaps it has to do with your parents, perhaps with other children, a teacher, or a situation that you felt powerless within.

Because children are essentially powerless, we all have those memories within us, memories that seem to reinforce our lack of control or authority over our lives. So don't look too deeply; let something emerge that just doesn't feel good.

Here are a few things to remember as you begin. If the memory is of an adult who hurt you, imagine that no matter how wrong their actions or words were, this was the best they could do in that moment. Their own history lay behind whatever they did, or said. And that despite what they did, their deeper intention was never about hurting you, but more about trying to ease their own pain.

Once a memory begins to surface, sit quietly. If you are comfortable with closing your eyes, then do it. Turn your attention into your body and notice whatever you may be feeling, as the memory emerges.

Notice any sensations, any emotions. Simply be present to them without trying to change or judge them. Be open to whatever you are experiencing.

See the memory clearly in your mind's eye. See the people involved. The situation.

What do you feel inside yourself as you revisit this moment in time?

Be very present to your feelings, without judging or suppressing them. You may want to push or try to breathe them away, but do your best to simply stay present and allow whatever is happening inside you.

As always, if you begin to feel overwhelmed or anxious, back off. We never want to go somewhere we aren't ready to go. Bring your awareness back to the room, back to your chair or whatever you are sitting on; open your eyes and take some deep breaths. Wait a few minutes, and see how you feel.

Perhaps just approaching the situation as far as you did was enough. Just by intending to change something painful makes a shift. Later down the road, you can come back to it and go a little further — or not. Listen to your body, gently respect your instincts.

If you do feel able to remain present and aware, then continue to move further into that moment long ago. Tune into all the sensory details of the experience. Sights, sounds, smells, touch — whatever your senses become aware of.

Be very present to your body. Your physical sensations. Your emotions.

What thoughts are going through your mind? Are they telling the same old story about this? Observe the viewpoint, but don't engage or continue to validate it.

Witness whatever you are experiencing without judgment or suppression.

It may take some time and your body may become very uncomfortable. At any time, you can stop the experience and return to this present moment, so don't go beyond your capacity to remain spacious.

If you can remain present and aware without going into full-on panic, then do so. Notice what your body feels like doing. It may feel like moving or shaking, or your limbs may twitch. Allow any small movements, any releases.

Our painful memories are literally energies that get trapped in our bodies and continue to influence our experiences — long past the moment, the environment, and even long past any of the peoples' presence in our life!

We must allow the energies to come forward, move, and ultimately disperse. Stay present, open, and spacious. Feel yourself as the expansive container within which energies can be transmuted. Become an alchemist, turning this dross from the past, into gold.

Finally, finally, you will find some calm. The storm of feeling and energy will ultimately subside.

There will be a new space, a potent emptiness, before you.

Take a moment, just to sit within this realm of possibilities.

Now you are ready for the revision process.

Start to explore different, more satisfying scenarios.

Try on a few different ones, noticing how you react.

Experiment with scenarios in which you are valued. Where the words, whether spoken to or by you, are appreciative and supportive. Where actions become kind and thoughtful.

Keep trying on different possibilities until you find one that resonates in a satisfying way. That feels like a deeply fulfilling alternate reality. Where discord has changed to harmony. Where upset, pain, or disappointment has become understanding and support.

Once you find a nourishing new scenario, play it out further in your mind's eye.

Feel it in your body. What sensations are you experiencing? What emotions are flowing through you?

Stay in this for a few moments. Notice how you feel and how the other person seems to feel. You may notice a sense of relief within them as well.

Expand this new scenario out into your history. Does it impact other memories for you? How does it affect other people involved?

Does this change anything for you in other aspects of your life? Not just your memories but even now, in your present time?

Continue to explore how this new scenario impacts your life. Like a ripple in a pond, watch the changes expanding out.

Take your time, don't rush.

Sit in the feelings, in the energy of this new story, this new reality.

Gently, when you are ready, open your eyes and return to the present. Look around you. Reacclimate.

Write down this new scenario, with as much detail as you can. Or draw a picture that represents this new reality. Dance it. Sing it.

Going forward, revisit this new-and-improved memory regularly, grounding it further within you. Notice any ripple effects this one transformation makes. When we change our stories, we change a great deal more.

Elevating Generations Through Love — My Story

Of course our parents weren't the source of all things gone wrong. They were simply the heirs of their parents' griefs and losses, sorrows and traumas — and their parents before them. What would happen if we lovingly revised stories back through the generations?

Here is some of my restoration work, again inspired by my father and the difficulties we once knew.

I was probably nine. We were visiting my grandparents (Dad's parents) in the summer, as we did every year. There would be dinner parties, with late nights and drinking. As the evenings progressed, louder voices, sometimes tears, sometimes yelling. Followed by tense mornings: my grandmother limping around the kitchen, overly solicitous to the three of us, with Grandpa long disappeared outside.

One afternoon I walked into Mom and Dad's bedroom, looking for my mother. She wasn't there, but on the dresser was her lipstick, which had always fascinated me. I picked it up, twisted it out and pushed it over my lips. Looking in the mirror, I was so pleased! I looked so pretty!

Suddenly I wanted Dad to see me, hoping he would be pleased and think me pretty also.

I wandered around and found him outside alone, on the patio. "Hi, Daddy!" I said bravely. He looked at me and his face suddenly darkened in anger.

"WHAT DO YOU HAVE ON YOUR FACE, YOUNG LADY? GO TAKE IT OFF RIGHT THIS MINUTE!" I was horrified, mortified, humiliated, shocked. Feeling I'd done the most terrible thing in the world, I ran to the bathroom and scrubbed the offending stuff off my face. For the rest of our visit, I stayed out of Dad's way.

Who knows what events get lodged inside us, quietly eroding our feelings of safety or self-esteem or lovability? That memory summed up how little Dad and I were connected throughout my childhood — but was it really about me?

Maybe there were discords and conflicts within him that kept him uncomfortable? Maybe distance was the only way he knew how to manage his own unresolved feelings?

As I have continued to approach past pain through love, one day the lipstick memory came up. My old yucky feelings were no longer attached, but instead I began to consider the source of Dad's distance. Why was he so stern and unavailable?

Sitting quietly, eyes closed, going into a place beyond time and space, I went back to my grandparents' house. The lipstick wasn't an issue for me anymore, but there was so much heaviness and pain around Dad when he went back to his parents' home. So much unspoken tension, he had to keep himself on a tight leash simply to make it through the visit.

His mother's possessiveness had long ago morphed into grasping demands—and her oldest son's stubborn independence only made her more desperate. Separation, neediness, rejection, there was a landmine of unacknowledged confusion between them that maybe spilled over into his behavior toward me.

And his father — downtrodden because he could never fulfil those endless needs, the demands for fine things, the balm for her anxieties — he had retreated into deafness and deference. No longer the father my dad remembered, but still the one he loved and wanted more for.

Now I saw a fuller scenario: myself, still a child, inside the house, looking out at him where he stood on the patio. I could feel his conflicts, his angst at being there, duty-bound but so tired of the dynamics, so resentful of his mother and her meddling, so disappointed with his father for putting up with it.

And then I saw Nona. Her pain in feeling excluded, set aside, abandoned, dreams long broken. My grandfather's painful impotence at not being able to fulfill her endless needs, ultimately handled by withdrawal from her, from his sons. Shutting up and putting up.

As I saw all these different aspects of their experience, frozen in a moment in time, so much became clear to me. Dad's standoffishness. Nona's tantrums. Grampa's humiliation. All the pain. All the confusion.

I felt such love flowing from my heart to them all. How can we ever hold anyone accountable, when they are drowning in the waters of dashed hopes and dreams? Of disappointment and confusion?

As I gazed through eyes of love, their straitjackets began to loosen; the thick walls between them began to crumble.

I saw the three of them — Dad, Nona, Grandpa — all growing taller, more upright, but looser at the same time. Their heads coming up, looking at each other. Moving closer to each other. The separations dissolving, the reaching out of their hands, the contact between them.

I continued to watch from inside the house, as the three of them stepped forward into a deep embrace. They stood with heads bent together and touching, arms around each other. All pretenses had dropped; nothing but resolution, restoration and love between them now.

The energy radiated out from their trinity, as the young me moved toward the patio, toward them. I walked out through the door and all three looked at me, huge smiles on their faces. "Susie." Their arms opened wide to include me in the embrace.

Finally: The gap had been bridged, the age-old energies shifted, the ancient wounds healed. In my world, and beyond.

Trust in Our Circumstances

Years ago, I read this story in a *Reader's Digest*. It was about a young woman who had been hiking in the wilderness and gotten lost. It was wintertime and darkness fell. She was exhausted, without enough clothes to stay warm or strength to build a shelter. No longer able to continue, she finally sank into the snow, certain she would perish during the night.

As she lay cold and shivering in the darkness, suddenly a large shape appeared next to her. It dropped down and settled into the snow, leaning right up against her. Emanating great heat, gradually its warmth permeated her as well. She nestled into its bulk and fell asleep, protected by the rising and falling of its breath and animal warmth.

When morning dawned, she awoke with the animal still there. As it grew light, she realized it was a large elk. With her stirring, the elk heaved its enormous body up and slowly walked away, disappearing into the forest. Now rested, the woman was able to get up and ultimately find her way back home.

That story struck a deep chord in me. No matter how far we may wander, how dire our circumstances, how tragic our situations, we are never truly lost or alone. There is a greater safety net — or story, or purpose — behind everything we experience, even when it doesn't seem to turn out that well from the worldly viewpoint.

We won't always have an elk lie down beside us, but beyond the surface experiences and outer progression of our lives is something profound and lasting. Something our worldly-focused minds cannot really grasp, although quantum physics and cutting-edge science have clued us into vast dimensions of beingness and creative possibility we seem to be a part of.

A human life is such a curious, ironic journey! Out of the infinite pool of creative energy, a "me" begins to emerge. A "me" whose initiation to earthly life is spent growing within a human body, encoded by and marinating within two different strains of human history.

And then we are born — through the perilous journey from inner to outer, from fusion to separation. Emerging while still completely helpless, immature and unprepared for external life, we must learn as quickly as possible how to adapt.

Who teaches us? Those still in the early stages of their own hero's journey; who have not yet fully understood, let alone mastered, the challenges set out for them. The teachings we absorb without question become our life's foundation: built upon a reality others believed in and that we, in turn, go onto accept as truth.

And so off we go, thinking we know how life works, and what we need to do within it. How's that been working out? Sometimes good, sometimes bad. Sometimes terrible!

Yet it is through the not-so-good or even terrible pitfalls, the moments of hurt or misunderstanding, that an elk can suddenly appear by our side; that can lead us to finding a right, even within a seemingly great wrong. That will reveal where we have been fueling our suffering, so we can finally start directing ourselves toward the kinder reality we are so worthy of.

The scope of this book has been mostly on a personal level. To come to see our own origins as being the seeds for individual transformation, for our singular hero's journey. When we understand our amazing bodies, brains, and energy systems — and use them deliberately — we harness our power to transform narrow, alienating limitations absorbed from the past.

No other species on this planet seems to embody such possibility for change.

When we decide we have had enough of blaming others, of holding them accountable for our own faults or disappointments; when we decide we have had enough of disliking ourselves, feeling unworthy, incapable, unlovable or any number of things we may have mistakenly believed; when we decide we alone are responsible for the perceptions and experiences of our lives, we can deliberately decide to cultivate a different attitude. We can practice withdrawing our energy from what we "know," and begin to project it into new territory. We can enter into the pursuit of personal mastery.

If we decided to project kindness to ourselves and others, how would that change our experience? Our reality? The reality of each and every person? Of each and every other inhabitant on our earth, whether human, animal, vegetable, or mineral?

It is a great question to ask. Could it be that the energetic blueprint we humans possess contains the means for not just our survival, but a new potential for humanity? That through the conscious utilization of our brain's and body's capacities, we could set in motion a new paradigm for life and the planet?

What would the human experience be like, if enough of us were so kind, so loving, that we could not do anything other than respect and be kind to each other?

We seem to be on a precipice in the world's history. If we continue to move in the same pattern of energetic frequencies we humans have been regurgitating these last millions of years, the conclusion for the future is questionable.

We cannot blame those from whom we come; that's just the state they were in. But now we know a different possibility exists. The key to unfolding a new future lies right inside of us.

We can reach to create new neural pathways, new beliefs about our goodness, our connectedness. It takes courage — and radical love — to do this. But if we truly take up the task, we can become the change we already see. We know how — we just have to remember. To re-member. To elevate.

Can you love yourself enough to re-member and elevate your life? To envision and empower peace with everything in both your present and your past? To lovingly release what no longer serves you? To question the beliefs that make you unhappy or angry or resentful or guilty or afraid?

Through us does life emerge. It happens through one small intention after another. We are so much more than we have known. We are all potential masters.

The Tao is called the Great Mother:
Empty, yet inexhaustible,
It gives birth to infinite worlds.
It is always present within you.
You can use it any way you want.[20]

I was in a village in the Indian Himalayas at a small meditation and hiking retreat. One night I woke around 2 a.m., my mind

[20] Lao-Tzu, trans. Stephen Mitchell, "Chapter 6," in Tao Te Ching: A New English Version (New York, NY: HarperPerennial, 1988).

relaxed. The days of contemplation and meditation had tuned my awareness away from beta-minded, external world chatter. I was open to mystery.

I lay there drifting, aware of myself and my surroundings, but receptive to whatever was waiting for me to discover. And suddenly I entered a full experience of Being. My consciousness was filled with a pervasive presence that was… Everywhere.

It was a presence connecting everything, flowing through oceans and mountains, deserts and cities, empty space and beyond. A vastness within which we were all contained, all held. That flowed through my veins, my organs, enlivening every cell in my body. Enlivening every molecule in the Universe.

As I realized this Presence, it was as if I was looking through its eyes. Divisions dissolved, time and space were like ocean waves continually coming forward, withdrawing, coming forward once again. The eternal dance of Infinity, evolving, changing, yet mysteriously also staying the same.

I saw the turning of the earth, the changing of the seasons, the disasters and triumphs, the births and deaths, all within this greater Wholeness. Nowhere was there "other;" nothing was separated from this All That Is.

Those things we humans worry about — our planet, our environment, our society, our family, our finances, the roof over our head, the clink we hear in our car — whatever! — all held within this permeating Presence.

As I both felt and saw beyond what my beta mind could ever comprehend, an energy became palpable. The presence flowing through everything was… Love.

THIS is what we come from. THIS is what sustains us. THIS is what we return to, whether in sleep, or conscious awareness, or death. Always here, always surrounding and enlivening us, beyond what language can ever fully express.

When I considered my own life's journey through the lens of this ever-inclusive, ever-present, ever-sustaining energy, I saw the hand of love behind every aspect. Not sadness or punishment or guilt or anger or anything that even hinted of "wrong." I saw that behind each moment, each day, had been the hand of... God. Of goodness beyond our worldly perspective.

All the challenges we face, all the hardships and harshness and destruction, even the most horrific human experiences, were included in this great continuing evolution.

My own hero's journey began to come into greater focus. The purpose behind the losses, the constriction, the diminishment, the fear, the pain, was never to keep me feeling small — but to give me the foundation from which something new and more fulfilling could grow.

No matter how harsh our origins may have seemed, none of us came to stay stuck in those limits. Our job as humans is to reach beyond our beginnings. We came to explore, to push, to fall down and then get back up. We came to let our lives point the way toward greater personal and collective fulfilment.

Can you see your life from this greater perspective? Where the challenges come forward not as impediments, but as pathways? Look at some of the themes running through your life. How many of them were set into motion through your origins? How have you grown and changed and evolved, as a result?

When we honor our difficulties in tenderness, we accept them as what they were always meant to be: vehicles for transformation and growth. Regardless of what the outside world thinks, we can restore a conscious ownership of our rightness. The rightness that we have always been, that holds and cherishes us, even when we have felt most forsaken.

Our human blueprint contains receptive channels to this recognition, but we have been "educated" away from it. We can't see or hear it; it has no form, so we are blind to just how beloved we truly are.

When we expand our awareness of ourselves — beyond our physical bodies, emotions, sensations, beyond what our beta brains can perceive — here is where Grace is found. The never absent, unseen connection permeating us, the world, and all within it.

We didn't come to these lives for a smooth ride, but to explore and evolve. When we accept our histories and experiences as being necessary friction for our transformation, nothing needs to be excluded.

This life, this human experience, will come to an end. Can you move forward through the time remaining within the perspective of rightness rather than wrong? Can you see all of your life through the eyes of love?

To find the origin,
Trace back the manifestations.
When you recognize the children
And find the Mother,
You will be free of sorrow.[21]

---

[21] Lao-Tzu, trans. Stephen Mitchell, "Chapter 52," in Tao Te Ching: A New English Version (New York, NY: HarperPerennial, 1988).

The Great Tapestry of You

True perfection seems imperfect,
Yet it is perfectly itself.[22]

Think about something you may have recognized, perhaps through the reading of this book, as being a major challenge to you. Perhaps a great disappointment or even trauma from your childhood. Or a painful situation you find yourself in now, that seems to have its roots in your past.

It could be something that has continued to eat at you or cause you to feel anger, resentment, sadness — or maybe something you hadn't even realized until now. Don't deliberately go digging; just take anything you remember about your childhood or aspect of your current experience, that you wish was different.

Think about it.

Make sure you are comfortable in your chair and close your eyes. Tune into your breath. If you feel some anxiety, know that you don't have to go anywhere frightening, you are completely free and in control to do this in whatever way is helpful and safe.

For now, just breathe and focus on your breath. Perhaps count your inhales and exhales, as we have done many times before.

---

[22] Lao-Tzu, trans. Stephen Mitchell, "Chapter 45," in Tao Te Ching: A New English Version (New York, NY: HarperPerennial, 1988).

Gently invite your inhales deeper into your body, but without stress or strain. Gradually begin to lengthen your exhales slowly and only as you are comfortable with.

This is your process; you are completely free to do what feels good, and refuse what doesn't. No one is forcing you. There is, in fact, nothing to "do" at all, other than relax and breathe.

If you feel like it, see the challenge you have recognized.
Go ahead and look at it.
See the people or place; see the whole scenario take shape.
If you visualize, then visualize it in detail.
If you have more of a feeling awareness, then feel what it is like.
Perhaps there are sounds — hear them.
Perhaps smells — smell them, once again.
Fill this out as completely as you choose — but again, only going as far as you want to go, in the process.

Notice what you are feeling within yourself.
What sensations are happening in your body.
What emotions are appearing.

Continue to breathe, allowing your breath to enter deeply, followed by the long, flowing exhales.

If you feel anxious, focus more on your breath, on the rising and falling of your abdomen, of the energy of the breath filling and emptying, again and again. Stay present to whatever you are experiencing.

Once you feel settled, imagine yourself moving up and back; discovering a higher perspective of the scene you have been viewing.

You can still see it, but you also see the long journey of your life from before that moment. All the living that came before.

All the moments that have happened since.

You see your whole life as a long journey, with that experience being just one single moment in it.

From this perspective, notice the influence that moment may have had.

Like a thread woven within the great tapestry of your life.

Like a refrain that repeats, in different variations, within a great symphony.

Like a challenge of mastery you have continued to approach, work on, and explore through your life.

A theme with many shades, many manifestations, circled again and again where you have continued to tug here and pull there; adjusting and working through knots; gradually seeking to smooth and integrate into the richness of this great tapestry.

Notice what you notice. Perhaps you will see the themes clearly. Perhaps you won't.

Whatever you experience, whatever you notice, is fine.

There is no hurry here, your journey is ongoing and the destination, whatever and whenever reached, is a continual unfolding of awareness, of realization.

From this height you can see a greater meaning to your life, to all that has happened within it. Even the most difficult, traumatic, or painful moments have a place within this tapestry, within this great symphony of YOU.

You are so much more than your beta-brained focus. Discover the awesome truth of you; witness the vast expanse your life contains.

Recognize your challenges as integral to the journey; as part of the evolution you came to experience, encompass, and grow through.

Perhaps you notice what is still unfinished, what you continue to work on. Allow and even celebrate those places. As long as we remain embodied here on earth, we are works in progress.

Notice where you have grown, where you have encompassed earlier challenges and found a greater wholeness through them. Where you have blossomed and expanded.

Notice as well where you are still in early growth, still green. Appreciate it all.

Appreciate this great adventure you are on, even as you still grapple with challenges you continue to call to yourself.

Appreciate yourself. Your embodiment. Your life. There is no one like you. Thank you for being here.

The Circle That Never Ends

In 2019, shortly after her ninety-fourth birthday, my mother breathed her last. She didn't go easily. The journey to that moment was a long, hard road she fought every step of the way, but ultimately her body called uncle and her soul took flight.

During my parents' final years, I flew between Vancouver and Houston frequently and eventually monthly. I was living two separate lives: my "real" life in Vancouver, paralleled by this alternate reality in Houston.

Mom had suffered many serious health issues over the years. Multiple times I'd had to drop my life and jump on a plane to handle a crisis. Waiting for the next shoe to drop was a constant reality.

Mom's last emergency was a bowel blockage when Dennis and I were traveling in rural Namibia. She was now ninety-three and had a list of chronic health problems as long as your arm, but this was acute and life-threatening.

Communication was challenging, but I managed to speak with her daily and be kept apprised of her condition. After a few days in the hospital, she was told that surgery was the only option. Given her frail health, this would be a gamble.

That night on the phone, Mom told me she decided to skip the surgery and go straight into hospice. I'd just have time to fly across the world directly to Houston before she passed.

While we had been away, our daughter Hanna had given birth to our first grandchild. I could hardly wait to meet him, but that would now have to wait. I'd go to Houston, be with Mom through her passing, and come home when I could.

In the middle of me figuring the logistics out, Mom spontaneously changed her mind. On my next call, I was astounded to discover she had undergone the surgery — and against the odds, had survived! Over the next few days, she mustered her strength yet again and gradually improved.

With this grace period, Dennis and I flew back to Vancouver, held beautiful little Archer, and then I hot footed it down to Houston.

Amazing! Mom was now in a recovery facility, and although weak, was completely herself! Frail yet still mentally alert, she, Dad, and I spent precious time together interspersed with going through their mail, paying the bills, touching base with the accountant and lawyer, and catching up on all the aspects of their lives that I had become fully in charge of.

Early on, the doctor pulled me aside. Although Mom had survived yet again, her other conditions were serious and terminal. Hospice was gently advised, and she agreed.

This time when she went back to their apartment, there would be no more heroic efforts to keep her alive. Surrounded by caregivers and nurses, she was kept comfortable as she declined both physically and mentally, and I continued my monthly commute.

Whenever I was there, her mind was clear; but in between, she started to hallucinate and go into different mental states, some of which were paranoid and even accusatory. She got mixed up about where she was living, about what was happening, about what others were doing.

And then she started seeing her mother. "Oh — Mother's here!" she would tell the caregivers, as she looked up into an empty corner of the room. The times of her long life were blending, overlapping, as she moved closer to taking her physical leave.

Yet whenever I spoke to or was with her, she returned to the here and now. I could still call her back to the reality where the rest of us remained focused.

A week after her ninety-fourth birthday, I got the call. She was entering her last days.

Flying down, I felt a sense of elation. I knew absolutely that death would be a sweet release from her emaciated and pain-wracked body. She had managed to keep herself going far longer than anyone would have thought, but those years had provided so many beautiful moments.

So many memories, some of which I'd never heard, had been shared. Openhearted communion had flourished. Nothing had been left unsaid, unshared, or unresolved. All that remained between us now, was love.

When I arrived, it was late in the evening. Mom and Dad were both in their beds. Dear Dad, now completely blind and innocent in his dementia, was sleeping like a baby while Mom lay in raspy unconsciousness. Meagan and Dovie, two of their faithful caregivers, greeted me with hugs then moved aside as I came over to Mom's bed.

Her wrinkled hand, long deformed from arthritis, lay on the covers and I gently picked it up. "Hi, Mom," I said softly. She must have heard or felt me through her unconsciousness, as she stirred.

Her eyes opened, gradually focused on me, and a shining recognition lit them up. She moved her mouth and tried to speak, but nothing came out.

Her eyes communicated her gratitude for all the years we had had together, the great joy our journey as mother and daughter had brought. I felt it and echoed every last note. We had precious moments together, me speaking with words and Mom through her loving gaze — until she sank back into the twilight of unconsciousness.

Her last words came later that night. Dad was being led back from the bathroom by his caregiver and he came to her bedside where I was sitting. We gave him her hand and he said, "Joan, honey."

His touch, his voice, brought her forward into consciousness one more time. Her eyes opened and when she saw him, that same great transmission of love shone through. She looked at him tenderly, smiled, and with great effort, whispered, "Night, night." And then, after a long, loving moment looking at us both, she went where we could not follow.

But she wasn't done with life quite yet. Mom hadn't met Archer. Remembering Stuart's death, she hadn't wanted Hanna and Mike to bring him down at too young an age. Now six months old, they were due to arrive in two days. She seemed determined to stick around until then.

Mom remained unconscious and unresponsive, conserving whatever she had left. She continued to breathe rhythmically and occasionally raise her eyebrows, while her caregivers and I took turns holding her hand, sitting, talking, and singing to her. She was waiting.

Two days later, her breathing now fast and shallow, Hanna walked in with Archer in her arms. "Hi, Grammy!" she said, "We're here! And here's Archer!" She touched Mom's unresponsive hand, and then put Archer's soft, warm little one on top of it.

And somehow, although nothing seemed to change, the whole atmosphere shifted. Her eyes remained closed, her breathing shallow, her body unmoving, but there was a palpable... Something.

To the outsider, Mom remained the same — unconscious, dying — but Hanna and I saw and knew her as we had always known her, and those precious last moments together on earth were permeated with an energy that felt... heavenly.

Archer was happy and laughing, while Hanna and I sang and joked and shared so many of our favorite stories and memories with Mom. It was her final, earthly gift to us: to celebrate — together — the exquisite sweetness of all we had shared in this lifetime.

There was no doubt: We knew she knew we were there; we knew she had been waiting for this final moment; and we knew she knew she could go now in peace. Which shortly thereafter, she did.

With Mom's death, I was shocked by the immensity of my grief. No matter how much I knew that death is simply another opening into a different reality, I ached. No matter that I knew she was now free of pain and suffering, her physical absence was an empty vacuum that brought me to my knees. I tried to talk myself through it, convince myself of her presence in other ways — a bird singing, a rose in bloom — but couldn't get over the stabbing pain of loss.

Those next days were the worst I've ever spent, as I started to do all that needs to be done after a death, along with helping Dad and the devastated caregivers — all of whom loved Mom as if she were their own.

Everything reminded me of her, but in the worst way. It was as if there was a hole in the world — a black hole — that had sucked out all of life's color, leaving behind nothing but a scorched wasteland.

After handling the immediate needs and making sure everything was in place for Dad, I returned to Vancouver and my "other" life at home. Distance helped a bit but the sorrow continued, appearing out of the blue to leave me gasping and in tears. I was shocked at how much I grieved her departure, despite knowing she had wrung every last drop out of her earthly time.

Three weeks after her death, I had a dream. I was sitting beside Mom's dead, lifeless body, which was lying on the bed just as she had been. I was occupied by some small tasks, nothing important but keeping me busy.

I briefly glanced over at her dead face, and of course it was immobile. But then, just as I was starting to look away, I thought I saw a slight movement.

Glancing over again, to my amazement, there *was* movement! I kept watching, astonished, as her whole face began to come alive! She was returning to life! While I continued to watch in disbelief, she opened her eyes. And saw me standing there. As we looked into each other's eyes, the biggest, broadest smile spread across her face.

"Oh, Mom!" I said, overjoyed and amazed! "I'm so glad to see you!" I thought for a moment, as I continued to drink in her presence, and then blurted out, "How *is* it?"

Eyes lit up with slow and steady joy, she gazed deeply into my own. And said, "Oh, Susie, it's WONDERFUL!"

And so I knew, beyond any further doubt. We come from love, and return to love. Anything in between is but a temporary illusion.

The Blessed Lord said:
Although you mean well, Arjuna,
Your sorrow is sheer delusion.
Wise men do not grieve
For the dead or for the living.
Never was there a time when I did not exist;
Or you, or these kings; nor will there come
A time when we will cease to be...
These bodies come to an end
But that vast embodied Self
Is ageless, fathomless, eternal,
Birthless, primordial, it does not die when the body dies.[23]

---

[23] Bhagavad Gita
A New Translation by Stephen Mitchell
Translate copyright 1988 by Stephen Mitchell reprinted by permission of Harpercollins
Copyright 2000 b Stephen Mitchell published by Harmony Books

ADDENDUM 1

What Are You Creating With Your Energy? Tune in — to Transform

Take a moment. Close your eyes. Tune into your body. Notice whatever you are feeling. Don't question, judge, or try to change — just become aware and present to your experience right this minute. Tune into your energy. Tune into the sensations in your body. The emotions flooding through you. The thoughts in your mind. Become very present to them. Like a detective. This isn't about anything other than discovering your energy, in this moment in time.

Whatever you discover, don't try to change it. Just notice how you feel. What your thoughts are saying. What your body is expressing. Become as open and present to yourself, without judgment, as possible.

Without changing anything, consider that right now, everything you are experiencing is like your own magic wand. This current state is how you are creating your future. Your energy right now is the determining force for your next moment.

Notice, even more carefully, the "pitch" or tone of your energy. Are you feeling more positively oriented, or are you tuned toward things that are wrong in your world? Are you anticipating your dreams and desires as possibilities, or are you feeling a sense of helplessness or pessimism?

Do you experience yourself as being fueled by a constant, positive energy — or left fending for yourself in a cruel, cold, chaotic world?

Or perhaps you notice something in between... Just notice, without trying to change anything. Be present to your present state. Without judgment.

Just tune in. Don't judge. This is about finding your energetic set point, the internal state that is literally creating your next experiences. It's not about beating yourself up, it's about getting some insight around the power you have, and how you are using it.

Your mind may start to throw out all sorts of arguments about how screwed up the world is. How wrong things are. Maybe it says some things about you. Your responsibilities. Pressures. Inadequacies — or the inadequacies of others.

Notice what happens in your body when you follow those kinds of thoughts.

Notice your physical sensations. Your emotions. Follow the cycle these thoughts set up throughout your physiology and neurology. Remain observant without trying to change anything. You are simply becoming conscious of how sensitive you are. How powerful you are.

Imagine — just a thought in your mind, and look what happens in your body. In your energy.

We are constantly creating — our thoughts, expectations, desires, beliefs, are forever manifesting something. It could be something within our bodies, it could be something out in the world. We are always using our energy to create.

This energy we have — its origins stretch back to before our birth. Before we had a physical body. Can you feel this energy within you? How it has been part of you for as long as you can remember?

Go back in your mind's eye... back through your life, through the experiences and choices and paths taken, and those not. Back through your teen years and childhood. Back through your family, the ones who raised and influenced you. Back to your mother who bore you, whose womb sheltered you. Back to before even that.

Back to the desire to come into this life. Nothing was forced, no one was making you. Can you feel any urge? Just be present to whatever you are experiencing, without judging. If you feel any inspiration, great. If you feel pure dread and disappointment, that's okay too. Even that will give you a sense of what direction your energy tends toward.

Come back to this present time in your awareness, keeping your eyes closed and your focus inward. Move forward in your imagination. Through the time still ahead of you in this life. The road still ahead.

What do you notice? What kinds of emotions or prospects do you see or believe in for yourself?

Notice whatever you are experiencing. It may not be pleasant — or you may feel excitement and joy. Whatever you are feeling is perfect, simply allow and accept it. We can't make ourselves feel or be anywhere other than where we are, right now. If your future looks and feels blessed, thank yourself for this. If it feels dark and depressing, thank yourself for this also. Be honest with where you are pointing your creative energies. And then ask yourself if this is a direction you want to keep yourself pointed towards.

Until we are conscious of where we are, nothing can be shifted. Just recognize where you are tuning your creative vibrations. If it's toward the energy of discontent, consider you are building a stronger manifesting energy in the direction of something that, while familiar, isn't that enjoyable.

How does it feel to focus your attention and energy on something unpleasant? Or on a subject that really gets you going?

Notice what happens in your body, the chemical signals that start to flow, the thoughts that continue to build up, the physical sensations that appear. And then notice what kind of reactions to these sensations, thoughts, and feelings start to emerge as the energy continues to flow in this direction.

What do you want to do? Punch a wall? Go back to bed? Dissolve into tears? Just notice. Notice the chain of reaction within yourself, simply to an energetic direction. Nothing has happened externally, yet your internal world is continuing to experience, create, and manifest, even if only within your own body/mind.

So now — take this inner experience a step further. If you bring this energy forward into the world, what kind of results are you creating? Both within your experience, as well as the experience of others? If you continue to further focus this creative energy, what are you contributing to, both within your own experience and that of the greater world?

OKAY. Just stay with yourself, present to your internal state. Whatever you are feeling, remain present. Maintain a neutral space, even in the face of any discomfort or negative emotion. Whatever you are feeling, allow it to have its space — but without judging, or getting pulled into it.

This is about discovering your own creative power and noticing how you tend to use it. Noticing what kind of energy you are perpetuating — and projecting out into the world. And no matter what you discover, it's all OKAY!!

Because although we live in time and space, your truth is far beyond this moment, far beyond the manner in which you are currently using/interpreting/creating reality. Reality is forever changeable, malleable. What you may be aligning and expanding in one minute, can be redirected. The choice is always ours.

There is nothing we cannot open ourselves to within ourselves. Nothing we need to project outward into the world or blame others for. We have the capacity — the spaciousness — to encompass anything and everything that this life can or has brought our way. Not that there aren't terrible things, for there are. Each of us, regardless of the situations in our lives, have experienced deep pain. Deep losses. Deep betrayals. Deep trauma.

This is the stuff of our lives, but also of our growth. Of our evolution. Our transformation. Some of us will take on challenges that others cannot imagine surviving. Some challenges will, in fact, catapult us out of this current life to be picked up by others, as our collective evolution continues beyond this moment in time.

We are always works in progress. Whatever you truly seek to discover or heal or transform within yourself, reach for it. You may think, *Who am I to do that?* You may think about your smallness or powerlessness or insignificance. You may think of what others have said or implied about you and that you believed. You may have held others as being the ones to describe and define you and your possibilities.

You may never have considered that within you is the stuff that makes new worlds; that you are seeded with courage and strength beyond your dreams. But this you are. If you are reading these words, then consider yourself called. Not to fix anything "out there," but to transform anything "in here" that holds you as less than.

Love yourself and the origins that brought you into this world. They have all contributed to making you who you are, and those influences are furthering you along your hero's journey. Release anything that makes you feel unworthy — including holding others accountable for your reality. Just because someone else was stuck in pain, doesn't mean you have to carry it forward.

We are all longing for wholeness, and yet it's always here, waiting for us to uncover it. When we accept our challenges as catalysts towards growth, expansion and fulfillment, when we let everyone and everything off the hook for their shortcomings, we can finally be free to be ourselves. And in that moment, we see, finally, that nothing has ever truly gone wrong.

ADDENDUM II

Understanding Brain Frequencies

Electrical activity emanating from the brain is displayed in the form of brainwaves. There are five categories of these brainwaves, ranging from the most active to the least active.

Gamma Brainwaves (32-100 HZ)

Gamma brainwaves are the fastest measurable EEG brainwaves and have been equated to "heightened perception," or a "peak mental state" when there is simultaneous processing of information from different parts of the brain. Gamma brainwaves have been observed to be much stronger and more regularly observed in very long-term meditators, including Buddhist monks.

Gamma was dismissed as "spare brain noise" until researchers discovered it was highly active when in states of universal love, altruism, and the "higher virtues." Gamma is also above the frequency of neuronal firing, so how it is generated remains a mystery. It is speculated that gamma rhythms modulate perception and consciousness and that a greater presence of gamma relates to expanded consciousness and spiritual emergence.[24]

---

[24] "A Deep Dive Into Brainwaves: Brainwave Frequencies Explained," Muse, March 2, 2021, https://choosemuse.com/blog/a-deep-dive-into-brainwaves-brainwave-frequencies-explained-2/.

Beta (13—30 Hz), 15—40 cycles/second When the brain is aroused and actively engaged in mental activities, it generates beta waves. Beta waves are characteristics of a strongly engaged mind. A person in active conversation would be in beta. A debater would be in beta. A person making a speech, or a teacher, or a talk-show host would all be in beta when they are engaged in their work.

Beta brainwaves are further divided into three bands; Low-Beta (Beta 1, 13-15Hz) can be thought of as a "fast idle," or musing. Beta (Beta 2, 15-22Hz) is high engagement or actively figuring something out. Hi-Beta (Beta 3, 22-32Hz) is highly complex thought, integrating new experiences, high anxiety, or excitement, associated with feelings of stress, paranoia, high energy, and high arousal. Continual high-frequency processing is not a very efficient way to run the brain, as it takes a tremendous amount of energy.[25]

Alpha (7.5-14Hz) — The Deep Relaxation Wave, 9 — 14 cycles/second

Alpha brain waves are present in deep relaxation and usually emerge when daydreaming or during light meditation. It is an optimal time to program the mind for success and it also heightens your imagination, visualization, memory, learning, and concentration. Alpha waves are the gateway to your subconscious mind.

Alpha is "the power of now," being here in the present. Alpha is the resting state for the brain. Alpha waves aid overall mental coordination, calmness, alertness, mind/body integration, and learning.

---

[25] Ned Herrmann, "'What Is the Function of Various Brain Waves,'" Scientific American, December 1997.

Theta (4-7.5Hz) — The Light Meditation & Sleeping Wave, 5-8 cycles/second

Theta brain waves are present during deep meditation and light sleep, including the all-important REM dream state. It is the realm of your subconsciousness and is usually experienced momentarily as you drift off to sleep from alpha or wake from deep sleep (delta).

It is said that a sense of deep spiritual connection and unity with the universe can be experienced in theta.

Your mind's most *deep-seated programs* are in theta, and it is where you experience vivid visualizations, great inspiration, profound creativity, and exceptional insight. And unlike the constant chatter of beta, the elusive voice of theta is a silent voice.

It is at the alpha-theta border, from 7Hz to 8Hz, where the optimal range for visualization, mind programming and using the creative power of your mind begins. It's the mental state in which you consciously create your reality.

Here, you remain conscious of your surroundings even while your body is in deep relaxation.

Delta (0.5-4Hz) — The Deep Sleep Wave 1.5 — 4 cycles/second

The delta frequency is the slowest of the brainwave frequencies. Delta waves occur in both deep, dreamless sleep and during transcendental meditation.

Delta is the realm of your unconscious mind and the gateway to the universal and collective unconscious. Information received here is often unavailable at the conscious level.

Deep sleep is important for the healing process as it aids with healing and regeneration. This is one reason why not having enough deep sleep is detrimental to your health.

Our brainwave profile and our daily experience of the world are inseparable. When our brainwaves are out of coherence, there will be corresponding problems in our emotional or neuro-physical health. Research has identified brainwave patterns associated with all sorts of emotional and neurological conditions.

Overarousal in certain brain areas is linked with anxiety disorders, sleep problems, nightmares, hypervigilance, impulsive behavior, anger/aggression, agitated depression, chronic nerve pain, and spasticity. Under-arousal in certain brain areas leads to some types of depression, attention deficit, chronic pain, and insomnia. A combination of underarousal and overarousal is seen in cases of anxiety, depression, and ADHD.

Instabilities in brain rhythms correlate with tics, obsessive-compulsive disorder, aggressive behavior, rage, bruxism, panic attacks, bipolar disorder, migraines, narcolepsy, epilepsy, sleep apnea, vertigo, tinnitus, anorexia/bulimia, PMT, diabetes, hypoglycemia, and explosive behavior.[26]

We are always projecting an energy field that covers an area beyond our physical body. We project a field and others are also projecting fields. One field can affect another field. Mostly no one has a clue that this is happening, except those people who have a stronger sensitivity to energy and some who can even see energy being emitted. For those of us without the visual ability, we may get a vibe from someone but rarely think about it in terms of energy. And while we may be quick to say someone else has "negative" energy, we don't necessarily question what our own energy field is emitting!

---

[26] "What Are Brainwaves?," brainworksneurotherapy.com, accessed July 26, 2022, https://brainworksneurotherapy.com/what-are-brainwaves.

References

Bright-Fey, J. *The Whole Heart of Tao: The Complete Teachings from the Oral Tradition of Lao-Tzu*. Birmingham, AL: Crane Hill Publishers, 2006.

Lao-Tzu, *Tao Te Ching: A New English Version*, trans. Stephen Mitchell, New York, NY, HarperPerennial, 1998.

Venema, Janita, *Presentchild: A Gift for You and Your Family*, trans. Jean Thompson, Haren: Homeolinks, 2012.

Bhagavad Gita, A New Translation by Stephen Mitchell Translate copyright 1988 by Stephen Mitchell reprinted by permission of Harpercollins Copyright 2000 b Stephen Mitchell published by Harmony Books

Acknowledgments

A book, like a lifetime, has so many influences, they cannot possibly all be named. My gratitude reaches throughout time and space to all whose energies have contributed to what is here.

Stephen Mitchell's exquisite translation of the *Tao Te Ching*, as well as Reverend John Bright-Fey's *The Whole Heart of the Tao*, a little book that literally fell off a bookstore's shelf into my hands some twenty-plus years ago, continues to deeply inform and direct my life, experiences, and explorations.

The people whose encouragement has been instrumental in the actual writing include Dr. Robert Pease, Barry Auchettl, Jeanne Zell, Oriane Lee Johnston, Brenda Pulvermacher, Carolyn Baker — and many more. Just because you may not be named, doesn't mean I am not aware and appreciative of your support.

My dear husband, Dennis, and daughters Hanna, Olivia and Lexi, who continue to inspire me in all aspects of my life. I am so grateful for our journeys together.

Sincere thanks to Karen Strauss and her team at Hybrid Global — including Dea Gunning, Michelle White, Karina Cooke — who have held my hand throughout the labor and birthing of this book.

And finally, to the many wise and wonderful clients, teachers, and friends whose generosity and trust have taught me so much. We are always learning from each other, regardless of which role we currently dance in. Thank you all.

CPSIA information can be obtained
at www.ICGtesting.com
Printed in the USA
BVHW051730060623
665489BV00016BA/1013